The Piccadilly Line

Desmond F. Croome

G000242064

Capital Transport

First published 1998

ISBN 185414 192 9

Published in association with the Piccadilly Line, London Underground Ltd, by Capital Transport Publishing, 38 Long Elmes, Harrow Weald, Middlesex

Printed by CS Graphics, Singapore

The front cover painting is by Peter Green, GRA

The maps are by Mike Harris

The back cover poster is copyright London Transport Museum

CONTENTS

The untypical entrance to Holborn station, where the facing material was coloured granite instead of the usual ruby-red terracotta. This is the High Holborn entrance. LT Museum

A New Line Takes Shape

In its layout, the Piccadilly Line is one of London's odder tube railways. It follows a great inverted horse-shoe across north, central and north-west London, so that a train facing south-east in north London can, later in the same journey, face north-west in west London. This curious configuration arises from the events of 1901, when three separate schemes were joined together in what turned out to be a master-stroke in a railway political battle.

In common with the national railway system, most of London's railway network arose from speculative investment, with the investors regarding a new railway as a means of yielding a satisfactory dividend. In practice, London's underground railways badly failed to live up to financial expectations. In a few cases, the main line railways gave underground lines a modest subvention for their role as feeders to the London termini, or to relieve pressure on bottlenecks, but such cases were exceptional.

Two technical developments allowed London's tubes to develop – the Greathead shield to allow deep-level tunnels to be driven through the London clay, and electric traction. These were first brought together in the City & South London Railway, whose first section opened in 1890, but yielded miserable financial returns. However, its technical success caused several tube schemes to be submitted to Parliament in 1892. Although they obtained parliamentary powers, they failed to attract investors.

Meanwhile, the Metropolitan District Railway, built on the cut-and-cover principle and operated by steam traction, was sinking ever deeper into the financial mire, and had not paid a dividend on ordinary stock for many years. In 1896 a group of shareholders arranged a survey for a deep level tube from Earl's Court to Mansion House, almost entirely beneath the District, and with an intermediate station at Charing Cross. New saloon-type bogie carriages would be hauled by electric locomotives from Earl's Court eastwards. At Earl's Court they would take over from the steam locomotives, which had brought the trains from the District's western branches. The scheme would have given a much quicker journey to the City, and would have relieved the most congested part of the existing District Railway. The Metropolitan District board approved the proposal, and obtained parliamentary powers in August 1897.

The second constituent of the Piccadilly was the Brompton & Piccadilly Circus, which was also approved in 1897. This was for a conventional tube between South Kensington and Air Street, just west of Piccadilly Circus, via Brompton Road, Knightsbridge and Piccadilly. The scheme included a power station at Lots Road, Chelsea (on the Thames) and a depot at Yeoman's Row, Brompton Road. A B&PC share offer in July 1898 was unsuccessful, and the company was acquired by the District in November of that year. Powers were obtained to join the District Deep Level at South Kensington, and to build the Deep Level thence to Earl's Court. Subsequent legislation modified the Deep Level at Earl's Court and extended the deep level line to a tunnel mouth west of West Kensington station. Access to Hammersmith was gained by widening the District cutting.

In North London, the Great Northern Railway's suburban services had encouraged extensive housing development in the inner suburbs. The main line was widened at great expense, and a suburban service of maximum possible frequency was provided. However, complaints continued to pour in, both from individual passengers and from deputations of season ticket holders. The crux of the problem was the bottleneck at Finsbury Park. The Great Northern & City scheme of 1892 would have given an extra through route from Finsbury Park to Moorgate, but no extra tracks at Finsbury Park station. The Great Northern fell out with the GN&CR, and instead gave moral support to the Great Northern & Strand scheme of 1898. This was for a new tube railway from Wood Green to Holborn, beneath Great Northern land as far south as King's Cross (with underground stations corresponding to those on the Great Northern) then cutting across the street pattern to Russell Square, then via Southampton Row to Holborn. The proprietors gained knowledge of a London County Council bill to clear old property and build new roads which were later named as Kingsway and Aldwych, and took advantage of this scheme to extend the proposed line to Wych Street, Aldwych. The application gained parliamentary approval, and the Great Northern & Strand Act of 1899 was for a railway with its southern terminus just north of the present Kingsway/Aldwych intersection. The power station would have been at Holloway and the depot at Wood Green. Despite main line moral support, the scheme lay dormant until an unexpected source of capital became available in 1901.

The injection of capital arose from the activities of the great American financier, C.T. Yerkes (1837-1905) who had made a fortune in brokerage, and investing in tramways and elevated railways in Chicago. He moved to New York in 1899, and acquired the authorised but unconstructed Charing Cross, Euston & Hampstead tube in September 1900, backed by wealthy and powerful American syndicates. This was followed by Yerkes' acquiring control of the District Railway in March 1901, and the Brompton & Piccadilly Circus in September 1901. Yerkes then devised a plan to amalgamate the Brompton & Piccadilly Circus with the Great Northern & Strand (which he acquired for £131,016) which was to be abandoned between Wood Green and just south of Finsbury Park. Finsbury Park terminus would be built and owned by the Great Northern, and powers would be sought for a link line between Piccadilly Circus and Holborn, so that Holborn-Aldwych would be worked as a shuttle service. This was approved by the Great Northern & Strand board in September 1901. The final major tube in the Yerkes group was the Baker Street & Waterloo, whose construction had ceased with the bankruptcy of its original promoters. This was acquired in March 1902.

There was a holding company for the whole group, initially the Metropolitan District Electric Traction Co. Ltd, established on 15th July 1901, which was reconstituted on 9th April 1902 as the Underground Electric Railways Company of London Ltd (referred to hereafter as the 'UERL'). Finance from the existing American sources (including the Old Colony Trust of Boston, Mass.) was insufficient, and Yerkes secured the help of the international bankers, Speyers, with offices in London (Speyer Bros, with (Sir) Edgar Speyer [1862-1932] as the senior partner), New York (Speyer & Co) and Frankfurt (Speyer-Ellissen). On 5th April 1902 Speyer Bros, Speyer & Co. and the Old Colony Trust signed an agreement to form a syndicate to deal in UERL shares. As a reward for their efforts in forming the UERL, these three bankers were collectively awarded £250,000 cash, a payment which ultimately had to be borne by the operating railway companies. Shares were sold in America, Great Britain, France, Germany and the Netherlands.

Meanwhile events in the world outside the Yerkes empire had begun moving quickly. The opening of the Central London Railway in July 1900 inspired a torrent of new tube schemes in all parts of London, and a Joint Select Committee of the Lords and Commons was appointed to make recommendations on the eleven major schemes which were due to be considered in the 1901 parliamentary session. Of these, only one was completely rejected (a B&PC extension from Piccadilly Circus to Bloomsbury). As the Committee did not report until 26th July 1901, it was too late for the bills to be considered in the 1901 session. Leave was given for them to be carried over to 1902. Of the 11 bills, one was rejected, one withdrawn to be replaced by more extensive proposals, three carried over intact and six carried over for consideration in parallel with additional proposals by the same proprietors.

For the 1902 parliamentary session, formal notice was given of no fewer than 32 bills involving tube railways. These were considered by two committees of the House of Lords. One, under Lord Ribblesdale, dealt mainly with north-south lines, and the other, under Lord Windsor, mainly with the more contentious east-west lines, i.e. those giving the City–Kensington–Hammersmith connection which had been recommended by the 1901 committee. One Ribblesdale bill directly concerned the Piccadilly group – the Great Northern & Strand Act allowed a diversion south of Finsbury Park, abandonment between Finsbury Park and Wood Green, amalgamation with the B&PC, and powers for the Great Northern to build Finsbury Park tube station. Proposals to extend to Temple station were refused after objections by landowners and the London County Council.

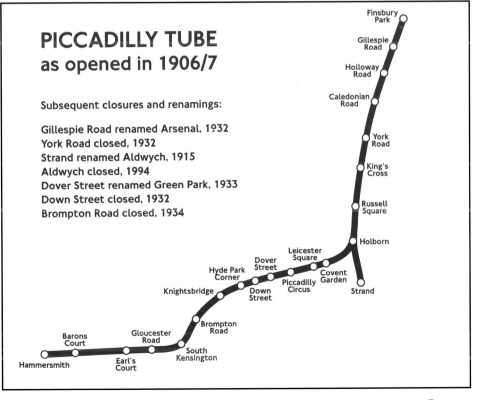

PICCADILLY TUBE
as opened in 1906/7

Subsequent closures and renamings:

Gillespie Road renamed Arsenal, 1932
York Road closed, 1932
Strand renamed Aldwych, 1915
Aldwych closed, 1994
Dover Street renamed Green Park, 1933
Down Street closed, 1932
Brompton Road closed, 1934

Finsbury Park
Gillespie Road
Holloway Road
Caledonian Road
York Road
King's Cross
Russell Square
Holborn
Leicester Square
Dover Street
Covent Garden
Piccadilly Circus
Strand
Hyde Park Corner
Knightsbridge
Down Street
Brompton Road
Gloucester Road
South Kensington
Barons Court
Earl's Court
Hammersmith

The Windsor Committee swiftly sorted out the various schemes for east-west lines, with the following results:

Brompton & Piccadilly Circus Railway. New lines sought, Piccadilly Circus – Charing Cross (District Deep Level connection) and South Kensington – Parsons Green refused. New line Piccadilly Circus – Holborn approved, also amalgamation with GN&S (to form the Great Northern, Piccadilly & Brompton Railway. Subsequently approved by Commons, Royal assent 18th November 1902).

Central London Railway. Existing line turned into a huge loop by extending from Shepherd's Bush to Hammersmith, then via Kensington, Piccadilly, Strand, Ludgate Circus to Bank, then a City loop, rejoining existing line at Old Broad Street. Refused on 16th May, (except for some very minor proposals) possibly on the grounds of avoiding the creation of a monopoly.

Charing Cross, Hammersmith & District Railway. Castelnau, Hammersmith, Kensington, Piccadilly, Strand. Refused on 13th May.

London United Electric Railways. Promoted by the London United Tramways, with loops at each end, one loop serving Shepherd's Bush and Hammersmith, the other Charing Cross and Victoria Embankment. Intermediate route via Kensington and Hyde Park Corner. A second, physically disconnected line would have linked Clapham Junction and Marble Arch. Branch from Hammersmith to Castelnau.

Piccadilly & City Railway. Hammersmith – Kensington – Piccadilly Circus – Charing Cross to Fleet Street/Salisbury Court. This line was backed by the powerful American banking and investment group headed by John Pierpont Morgan, a multimillionaire.

North East London Railway. From Fleet Street (Ludgate Circus) via Bishopsgate, Dalston, Stamford Hill and Tottenham to Southgate. This was another Morgan promotion.

During the course of the parliamentary hearing, these last three were amended. There were negotiations between the London United and the Morgan group, and the London United withdrew the section between Castelnau and Hammersmith and all lines east of Hyde Park Corner. The Piccadilly & City was abandoned west of Hyde Park Corner, where it would instead make an end-on junction with the LUER. At the other end, there would be a similar junction with the NELR, so that there would be a through route between Hammersmith and Southgate. These two were formally amalgamated into the Piccadilly, City & North East London Railway, and the whole scheme was known as the London Suburban Railway. Except for Southgate–Palmers Green (which impinged on Southgate cricket ground) this scheme was approved by the Windsor Committee and passed to the House of Commons. This house was anxious to ensure that the whole line was built, and instructed the Commons committee to take security from the promoters that the whole scheme of railways would be completed. After the Commons had begun to hear the LUER bill (and rejected the Shepherd's Bush loop) it adjourned for the summer recess. Unfortunately the Morgan group did not ensure that its allies were kept happy, and by summer 1902 the two parties fell out over the proportion of control that each would exercise over the management of the joint undertaking. On 28th July George White, Chairman of the LUT, proposed a new management agreement, but the Morgan group would not consider it. White was very annoyed, and in September 1902 sold his majority holdings in the ordinary shares of the LUT to Speyer Brothers. When the parliamentary hearing resumed on 21st October, counsel for the LUER announced that he wished to withdraw the Knightsbridge–Hyde Park Corner section of that bill, as it duplicated the Brompton and Piccadilly Circus, which would be prepared to make connections to restore the through route. The

Commons committee ruled that this contravened the Commons instruction, and the LUER bill was formally withdrawn. There were desperate attempts to recommit the LUER bill in the names of the Morgan syndicate, but to no avail, and the whole Morgan scheme was dead. MPs, British financial houses and journals expressed their severe disapproval of this outcome, but felt that it had been inevitable when American interests and methods were introduced to London.

The London & Suburban debacle brought to a head the general disquiet about the adequacy of the private bill system for authorising railways, and the lack of co-ordinated planning, control and supervision. Early in November 1902 the Government announced that a Royal Commission on London Traffic would be appointed, which took effect on 9th February 1903. The Commission reported on 17th July 1905. Its main recommendation was the appointment of a London Traffic Board to examine all bills affecting transport in Greater London, to try to make them harmonise with a general plan. Back in 1903, an official warning had been given that no major schemes for London railways could be considered until the Commission had reported. However, a few minor schemes were approved, including the tidying-up of the alignment and legal arrangements for the South Kensington–Hammersmith section of the GNP&BR (Acts of 1903 and 1904), an improved junction at Holborn, and an extension at Aldwych to Surrey Street/Howard Street (1905). In 1905 the UERL made a formal agreement with the Central London that neither side would promote a bill for a major east-west line in the 1906 session; by the end of 1906 the low traffic on new or electrified lines, and the increasing competition from mechanised road transport, had concentrated managerial minds on meeting the expenses of existing railways. Promotion of major lines across central London was deferred for several decades, and never again would such schemes be built by free-standing private enterprise.

Physical construction began with the acquisition of station sites, property demolition and sinking vertical shafts. The first Piccadilly construction sites were at Knightsbridge and South Kensington (April 1902), followed by the GNR's beginning its Finsbury Park low-level works in September 1902. By April 1903 twelve out of twenty station sites were in possession and there was a segment dump and shaft at Cromwell Road, Kensington. By February 1904 all station sites had been acquired, and boring the running tunnels was proceeding, 80 per cent having been completed by October 1904.

Tunnelling followed the same general procedures that had been developed on the City & South London. Vertical shafts were sunk from station sites until they were well into the stratum of London clay. These were lined with cast-iron segments and subsequently used as lift or ventilation shafts, or for spiral staircases adjoining the lifts. At the foot of these shafts the tunnelling shields were assembled, and began to move horizontally to construct the running tunnels. The Greathead shields were essentially metal drums with a circular cutting edge at the front, which were propelled by a ring of hydraulic rams bearing against the last completed section of tunnel. The circular tunnels were formed of successive rings of flanged cast iron segments, each segment being bolted to its neighbour in the ring and to the next ring. The twin running tunnels were 11ft 8¼ins internal diameter. A diameter of up to 12ft 6ins had to be used on curves to allow for the throwover of the bogie cars. Progress was accelerated by using the Price Rotary Excavator, based on a Greathead Shield equipped with a central shaft on which the rotating part was mounted. Six radial arms extended from this shaft, to which knives were fixed at different radii. When the arms were rotated by an electric motor and gearing, the knives cut grooves in the face of the clay, and buckets on each arm collected the clay and dropped it into a chute at the top.

Station tunnels were 350ft long and 21ft 2½ins internal diameter. There was a separate platform and tunnel for each direction. The standard arrangement was for the two platforms to be on the same level, connected by cross-passages served by stairways. These linked with further passages from the lower landings of the lifts.

The Great Northern & Strand Act of 1899 had a clause that delayed the construction of the tunnels at Holborn, and thence to Aldwych (named 'Strand' until 1915) until the LCC consented and the new road (Kingsway) was completed. An agreement was made with the LCC in June 1905, but these tunnels were delayed compared with the rest of the line, where the tunnels were completed by October 1905 and the permanent way was being laid. By July 1906 the main line tunnels were ready, the track and conductor rails complete except for a stretch at Covent Garden, and the construction of the lifts, stairways, ventilation plant and station buildings was well advanced. Substations were complete and equipped, except at Hyde Park Corner. The gigantic power station, on the bank of the Thames at Lots Road, Chelsea had been started in March 1902, and came into partial use on 1st February 1905. It was planned to supply the three UERL tubes and the electrified District, but the generating capacity was later expanded to feed part of the London United Tramways, and the City & South London and Central London Railways, securing economies by closing the smaller power stations.

In August 1905 the UERL bought two Hurst Nelson battery locomotives and 10 flat cars. These worked on the construction of the Piccadilly and Hampstead lines, removing spoil and bringing in supplies of segments, rails and other equipment. After completion they were used for permanent way trains or hauling tank cars for emptying drainage sumps.

In the 'Alice in Wonderland' organisation of the Yerkes group, the UERL were technically the 'contractors' and the real contractors who performed the construction work were 'sub-contractors'. The Piccadilly tunnelling was divided between Walker Price & Reeves (Finsbury Park to South Kensington) and Walter Scott & Middleton (South Kensington to West Kensington), with Bott and Stennett building the tunnel mouths and the open-air section of line.

Far away to the west, in the open country north of Acton, the Ealing & South Harrow Railway had been completed at the end of 1899, and acquired by the District in 1900, but not opened because of the District's financial problems. The existing District line between Mill Hill Park (now Acton Town) and Hanger Lane Junction and all the Ealing & South Harrow were electrified by March 1903 to allow trials to be made in running the first District electric trains. This gave practical experience with the four-rail dc electrification system and the automatic signalling. There was a temporary power station on the canal bank at Alperton. Public service began from Mill Hill Park to Park Royal on 23rd June 1903 and to South Harrow on 28th June 1903.

In the summer of 1905 Yerkes' health began to fail. He was able to take the chair at the UERL board meeting on 10th October and the general meeting a fortnight later. In November he sailed to New York for a business trip but suffered a recurrence of kidney disease and died on 29th December 1905, aged 68. On 3rd January 1906 Sir Edgar Speyer was appointed chairman of the UERL, and Sir George Gibb, hitherto general manager of the North Eastern Railway, as deputy chairman and managing director.

The Yerkes group had early appreciated the importance of keeping the fourth estate fully informed of all developments. At 11.00 on 12th December 1906 a special train for the press left Hammersmith, picked up at Knightsbridge and Leicester Square,

One of two battery locomotives supplied by Hurst Nelson & Co Ltd in August 1905 for use in constructing the Piccadilly Line, and later the Hampstead Line. They were written off in 1918.

and then ran non-stop to Finsbury Park. On return it stopped at Holloway Road for an inspection of the spiral passenger conveyor installed there, and at Russell Square for the substation. The pressmen were then entertained to lunch at the Criterion Restaurant, entertained to a long speech by Gibb and a short one by Sir Edgar Speyer, and finally sent away with their handouts.

Finally came the great day when the Piccadilly would begin to produce some traffic receipts for the depleted UERL coffers. On Saturday 15th December 1906, David Lloyd George, President of the Board of Trade, came to Hammersmith. He was handed a golden controller key to start the 'first' train but it would not fit. A 'call examiner' (on the mechanical engineering staff) offered to file the key, but was instructed to lend his own to Lloyd George. The train then proceeded to Finsbury Park and back to Piccadilly Circus for lunch at the Criterion. Speeches were made by Sir George Gibb, Lloyd George and Sir Edgar Speyer. The general public were admitted as soon as the official party had left Piccadilly Circus station, and by the time that the lunch guests dispersed Sir George Gibb was able to announce that 9,500 passengers had been carried in the first two hours. (Empty trains had been running, for staff training and to test the equipment, since the end of October).

The opening had been hurried forward to catch the Christmas rush although some stations were not ready. These followed in 1907, with South Kensington on 8th January, Dover Street on 15th March, Covent Garden on 11th April and Aldwych on 30th November.

In the first few years, the volume of traffic on all these new tubes was far lower than had been forecast, which nearly brought about the downfall of the UERL. This story, and a detailed description of the line and its equipment, will be related in the next chapter.

Hammersmith to Finsbury Park

On the tube section of the Piccadilly, the Central London Railway's practice was adopted – whenever possible – of having uphill gradients into stations and down gradients on departure. The slopes were, in this case, of 1 in 66 up and 1 in 33 down, thus enlisting the force of gravity in braking and acceleration. The running tunnels were equipped with electric lights at 42ft intervals, supplied at 220V from substations. These were kept on continuously at first, but later during service disruptions only.

The track was laid on chairs attached to Australian karri-wood sleepers, which rested on a central concrete bed, with granite cubes under the sleeper ends. The bullhead running rails weighed 90lbs per yard, and were about 45ft long. Inside tunnels, the conductor rails were rectangular, weighed 85lbs per yard, and rested on earthenware insulators fastened to the sleepers. The negative rail was in the centre, $1\frac{1}{2}$ins above the running rails, and the positive rail 3ins above and 16ins outside one of the running rails (its position could be either on the left or right according to local requirements).

The conductor rails were energised so that the difference between positive and negative was about 550V dc. They were supplied by cables running from substations at Holloway, Russell Square and Hyde Park Corner, and from District substations at South Kensington and Earl's Court. The 11,000V ac supply from Lots Road power station was converted to a lower voltage by static transformers and to direct current by rotary converters.

The need to house the lift machinery in an accessible position dictated the layouts of the street-level station buildings on the tube section. The architect Leslie W. Green devised a standard layout which was adapted to the shape of individual sites. There was a large ground floor to house the ticket office, staff accommodation and the lift upper landings, whilst the mezzanine floor, which housed the lift motors and winding and control gear, had large glazed arches and small circular or rectangular windows (in a few cases large rectangular windows). The roofs were flat so that extra storeys could be added for commercial occupation. The structure was of steel clothed in brick, faced on the street elevations with glazed ruby-red terracotta blocks. In most cases the external station name was embossed in the tiles in Roman letters and picked out in gilt, displayed at mezzanine level, but at a few stations the name was in black sans-serif letters on white. Station lighting, both at surface and platform level, was by Maxim arc lamps and incandescent bulbs.

Between surface and lower levels there was usually an 18ft shaft with a spiral iron emergency staircase, and one or more 23ft shafts, usually equipped with two lifts. Russell Square was unique on the Piccadilly in having three lifts in a 30ft diameter shaft (although the Bakerloo had such shafts at Great Central and Oxford Circus). The number of lifts at each station varied from two to five, and the line had a total of 60 electric lifts supplied by the Otis Elevator Company under a comprehensive contract with the UERL. The ticket halls were tiled in green up to shoulder height, white above, and the ticket office windows had moulded tile surrounds in the Art Nouveau style.

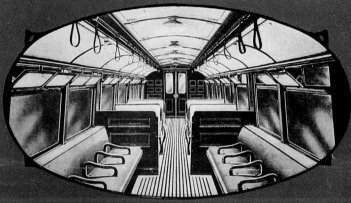

G.N., PICCADILLY, & BROMPTON

ELECTRIC RAILWAY
LONDON'S LATEST TUBE

QUICKEST ROUTE Between
NORTH & WEST
THROUGH THE THEATRE & SHOPPING AREAS

| Frequent Service. | Cheap Fares. |

STATIONS

FINSBURY PARK	HOLBORN $	KNIGHTSBRIDGE
GILLESPIE ROAD	COVENT GARDEN	BROMPTON RD
HOLLOWAY ROAD	LEICESTER SQUARE	STH KENSINGTON
CALEDONIAN RD	PICCADILLY CIRCUS	GLOUCESTER RD
YORK ROAD	DOVER STREET	EARLS COURT
KING'S CROSS	DOWN STREET	BARON'S COURT
RUSSELL SQUARE	HYDE PARK CORNER	HAMMERSMITH

PASSENGERS AGENTS OFFICE
42, HAYMARKET.

Advert for the new Great Northern, Piccadilly & Brompton Railway published at the time of its opening. The Great Northern element was the interchange provided at Finsbury Park.

Left **A commercial photograph of King's Cross northbound platform in 1906.**

Right **The surface buildings of King's Cross (Piccadilly) station, shortly after the Hampstead tube opened in June 1907. The Venetian windows between the arches were unique for a Leslie Green station.** LT Museum

The platforms were decorated in a unique tiling scheme that was applied to all 43 deep-level stations in the Yerkes group. A detailed description would be beyond the scope of this work, but the general scheme was for the platform walls to be decorated with 9in x 3in glazed earthenware tiles from the platform floor to about 7ft 6ins high. From floor level upwards there were, in succession, a band of coloured tiles to form a 'plinth'; a band of white, cream or yellow tiles; a few courses of coloured tiles forming a waistband; another band of plain tiles, and finally a frieze repeating the colours of the waistband. Vertical bands, 2½ tiles wide, sprang from the plinth upwards round the platform vault to end in a strip of tiles on the tunnel side at train roof level. The bands divided the platform walls into panels. Those above the waistband accommodated the station names, fired into the tile surfaces in dark brown letters, five tiles high. In the remaining spaces between waist and frieze were coloured geometric tile patterns, each station having a unique pattern. The untiled spaces (i.e. mainly the ceilings) were finished in painted plasterwork.

Apart from the station layout variations imposed by site restrictions, other variations derived from railway politics and geography. The two station tunnels that formed Finsbury Park terminus and the running tunnels themselves for about 300 yards south had been built by the Great Northern Railway, which charged rent to the Underground group. The station tunnels were lined with tiles, dark green below the waist, white above. The only lifts were four Musker hydraulic machines from the tube platforms to a circulating area beneath the GNR platforms. Passengers to and from the street had to use stairways debouching into a network of three street-level subways cut out of the main line embankment. The ticket office was at the head of the entrance stairway. Gillespie Road also lacked lifts, and passengers had to climb a long, sloping passage to reach the street level buildings. At Holloway Road, one shaft housed what was called a 'double spiral continuous moving track' to convey passengers on a moving belt of teak slats. However, it never entered passenger service, and most of it was scrapped in 1911. Some parts remained below the level of the lower lift landing, and these were selectively removed to the London Transport Museum in 1993. Caledonian Road and York Road were to the normal layout, except that the station tunnels were further apart than usual, so that there was room for the lifts to descend to platform level instead of a subway above the tunnels. (This special layout also applied at King's Cross and Earl's Court.)

King's Cross had the normal lifts and buildings with an interchange subway at subsurface level to the Metropolitan station (then on King's Cross Bridge) and a deep-level subway to the City & South London. At Holborn the platforms were on two levels. At the higher level was the main eastbound platform and that for the Strand shuttle service, connected by cross passages. The two tracks connected at a trailing junction just north of the station. The westbound platform, at lower level, curved west immediately south of the station and crossed below the eastern and western Strand branch lines. The latter had its own, shorter, Holborn platform. South of both branch line platforms there was a facing crossover, and both tracks continued in separate tunnels to Strand.

Back on the main line, Covent Garden was a bare 0.16 miles from Leicester Square (originally intended to be named Cranbourn Street). The last-mentioned station shared a surface ticket hall and five lifts with the Charing Cross, Euston & Hampstead Railway, but at Piccadilly Circus the Piccadilly line at first kept its ticket office and four lifts separate from the Bakerloo, because of constraints imposed by the deep level layout. Both these stations had deep level interchange subways. Dover Street and Down Street had their surface buildings hidden in side streets off Piccadilly, but Hyde Park Corner (St George's Place) was on the south side of Knightsbridge, west of the road junction. Knightsbridge (Sloane Street) in Brompton Road east of Hoopers Court, had some florid floral decoration in the tiles on each side of the arches, and a rear entrance in Basil Street. Brompton Road was on the north side, near the Oratory. South Kensington had the rudiments of a flying junction with a future District Deep Level line towards Mansion House, for which a short extra platform was built at the same level as the westbound Piccadilly. The eastbound platform was 18ft higher, and the lifts stopped at each platform level. Both here and at Gloucester Road the Piccadilly had its own station buildings, next to the District Railway's, but at Earl's Court, Barons Court and Hammersmith, the ticket halls were shared with the District. Barons Court, opened by the District on 9th October 1905, had two open-air island platforms, the northern one used exclusively by the Piccadilly, and the southern by the District. At Hammersmith, the Piccadilly had a separate two-track terminus, with the platforms covered by a low sloping glass roof. The centre platform was for passengers boarding the trains and the side platforms for arrivals. Interchange with the District was available at the western end near the ticket barrier.

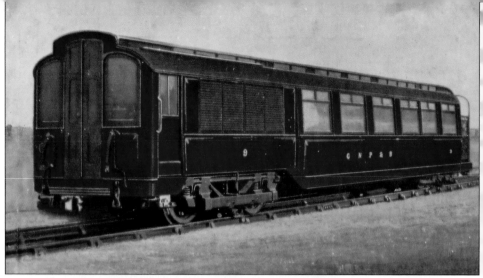

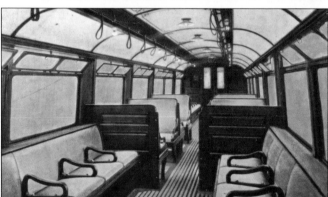

Top **French gate-stock motor car, illustrating the large proportion of car length occupied by the equipment compartment.**

Left **The interior of a trailer car, wih its rattan seating.**

As mentioned earlier, an automatic signalling system had been used on the Ealing & South Harrow Railway in 1903. This was developed from the pioneer installation of 1901 on the Boston Elevated Railway. Trains normally signalled themselves automatically, so that the only manned signalboxes were at junctions, termini and regulating points. Signals were normally in the 'line clear' position, but occupation of a track section by a train allowed the detecting current to flow through its wheels and axles. This change in electrical voltage caused the adjacent track relays to change the signal some way behind the train to 'danger', subsequently returning to 'clear' when the train had moved forward and occupied another track circuit. The tunnel signals originally comprised single lamps behind separate red and green spectacle plates which were moved up and down by compressed air. There were air-actuated semaphore signals on the open section, but all signals were eventually replaced by colour lights with separate lamps for each colour. The standard arrangement was a two-aspect stop signal, but repeaters were installed on sharp curves, 400ft before the main signal. Signalboxes were at Finsbury Park, York Road, Holborn, Covent Garden, Hyde Park Corner and Hammersmith. There were scissors crossovers before each terminus, and single crossovers at York Road, Covent Garden, Hyde Park Corner and Barons Court.

The main rolling stock order was shared equally between French and Hungarian manufacturers, Les Ateliers de Construction du Nord de la France, (Blanc Misseron) and The Hungarian Railway Carriage and Wagon Works (Györ or Raab). There were 72 motor cars, 72 trailers and 72 control trailers (trailers with driving apparatus at one end, enabling short trains to run at less busy times). Two British-made trailers had been delivered in autumn 1905 but were too large for the tunnels, and languished in the depot. The 216 cars were normally marshalled into 72 three-car sets, each consisting of motor-trailer-control trailer. All the trailers (measuring 50ft 2ins over buffers) had platforms and inward-opening lattice gates at each end. The motor cars (50ft over buffers) had gates at one end and a driving cab and equipment compartment at the other. The trailers had central blocks of transverse seats for 16 passengers, and groups of 18 longitudinal seats at each end. On the motors there were transverse seats for 24 passengers next to the equipment compartment, and longitudinal seats for 18 at the trailing end. All seats were upholstered in yellow rattan (the stems of a climbing palm tree), durable but cold to touch. On the longitudinal seats, each passenger space was delineated by wooden dividers. The steel-bodied cars had clerestory roofs and pairs of hinged quarter lights above the large fixed windows. Leather straps for standing passengers were attached to wooden rails fixed to the lower edges of the clerestory roof. Glazed double sliding doors were fitted. Lighting was by incandescent bulbs along the centre line of the car ceilings, with groups of five 120V lamps in series, drawn directly from the traction supply.

A French-built trailer car of the original order, showing the gated ends. LT Museum

The motor bogies were mounted under the equipment compartment, where the floor was higher than in the saloons. Two motors were fitted in each cast steel bogie. The multiple-unit system was used, so that the driver controlled the motors of his own car and those of the rear car. At the non-driving end of the motor car was a low-slung trailing bogie, allowing a floor height of only 1ft 10ins above rail level. The trailer cars had two similar unmotored bogies. Externally the cars were painted overall in crimson lake, and this rather unexciting livery was reflected by the internal fitting of fireproofed mahogany veneer. More cars had been bought than required by the scheduled frequency. Initially, 35 new cars were stored out of service, but were brought into use as traffic developed, some being transferred to other lines in the Underground group.

The car depot was at Lillie Bridge, Fulham, on the site of the old District Railway steam shed and repair shops. Its 78ft 6ins width allowed six parallel tracks, and it was nearly a quarter of a mile long. Access to the depot was most awkward. A connection just east of Barons Court led to two Piccadilly sidings north of the ramp to the tunnel. These connected with the eastbound District line west of West Kensington station, and east of the station was a single-track curved, sloping connection to the depot.

Gate stock trains made heavy demands on staff resources, and each interface between cars was manned, with the guard (or conductor) standing on the gangway plate between the first and second cars, and gatemen being similarly positioned between the other cars, making four gatemen and one guard on a six-car train. Fortunately the Piccadilly was able to have only one man in the driver's cab, because of the 'dead-man's' vigilance device in the controller handle.

Too much running time had been allowed for the through journey, and this was reduced from 38 to 33 minutes by October 1907. Traffic was so poor that three-car trains could be run all day (October 1908) except for six-car in the evening theatre rush. In that month there were 30 scheduled trains in each peak hour, and 20 per hour in the off-peak. Train lengths were gradually increased in accordance with traffic volumes. The fares were based on journey distance, and varied from 1d to 4d.

Passengers were generally obliged by economic circumstances to seek the cheapest route, and journey time was of less importance. Reliable electric trams and motor buses began to appear at just the wrong time for the new tubes, and in its first full year the Piccadilly carried under 26 million passengers instead of the estimated 60 million. Early returns from the Bakerloo and Hampstead tubes, and the electrified District, were equally lamentable. New management talent was needed to reverse the UERL's rapidly declining fortunes. The youthful Frank Pick took the route south from the North Eastern in the same year as Sir George Gibb, but the job change with the greatest long-term significance was the acquisition of A.H.Stanley (later Lord Ashfield) from the Public Service Corporation of New Jersey, USA in February 1907. He took on his general manager's duties in London in April 1907.

Gibb and Stanley threw themselves enthusiastically into developing ingenious ways to increase net revenue. Co-operation with other London railways yielded selective fare increases (including abolishing the Central London's 2d flat fare from 1st July 1907), through bookings and imaginative joint publicity. Services were improved, including trains which ran through some intermediate stations without stopping. Last trains from central London were standardised at 01.00, and passengers were also attracted by discounted strip tickets. All these measures gradually helped to turn round the company's fortunes. On the financial side, bankruptcy of the UERL was narrowly averted by the financial support of Edgar Speyer (appointed Chairman of the UERL in January 1906) and his associated banking companies.

Provision was made for development above the station buildings in many cases, as shown here at Gloucester Road in a photo taken 22 years after its opening. This station looks much the same today as can be seen in the view on page 75. LT Museum

Some limited prospective economies lay with the amalgamation of the three UERL tube lines. There had been proposals in the 1903 bills to transfer the Bakerloo and Hampstead to the Piccadilly, but these were withdrawn because of the appointment of the Royal Commission on London Traffic. Another attempt was made in 1906, when an amalgamation bill was proposed for the 1906-7 parliamentary session. This time it was the associated American bankers who killed the proposal, as they felt that it would depress the value of the tube shares when ultimately marketed. Three years later, the American opposition had been overcome, and the London Electric Railway Amalgamation Bill received royal assent on 26th July 1910. The Bakerloo and Hampstead merged with the Piccadilly, under the name of the London Electric Railway. The amalgamation was back-dated to take formal effect from 1st July 1910. It brought benefits to the travelling public in the reduction of some single fares, and the wider availability of workmen's return tickets. The three lines continued to be publicised under their separate names, and the man in the street would hardly have known of any change.

The Underground's first two escalators were installed at Earl's Court in 1911 to link the Piccadilly platform level with a circulating area beneath the District platforms. They were available from 4th November 1911, and were of the 'shunt' (or step-off-sideways) type, known internally as the 'A' type. From 1912, escalators were installed in all new deep-level stations, and subsequently most of the heavily-used deep level stations were converted from lifts to escalators.

The LER obtained powers on 15th August 1913 to link the Piccadilly Line at Hammersmith to the London & South Western Railway's Kensington – Richmond branch at Studland Road junction, west of Hammersmith, with the intention of running Piccadilly trains to Richmond, but this scheme was scotched by the outbreak of war.

Traffic Growth

Great Britain declared war on Germany on 4th August 1914 and the country gradually had to adjust. The drain on manpower obliged the Underground to employ women on many jobs normally done by men. Munitions manufacture took priority, and no new Underground rolling stock was made. Even maintenance had to be reduced. Higher wages but fewer goods in the shops caused inflation, which had an unexpected but ultimately beneficial effect on the Underground.

The District came under Government control, but the tubes did not, so it was the only Group railway that could pay its staff war bonuses. In order to put all railway staff on an equal footing, Albert Stanley obtained Board of Trade approval for a Common Fund, covering the District, the LER, the CLR, the CSLR and the London General Omnibus Company. Each company would pay its net receipts into a pool, after deducting working expenses (including war bonuses), interest, and dividends on prior stocks. The pool was then distributed in agreed proportions to the five companies. The LER portion of the fund, which was sanctioned by Act of Parliament and operated from 1st January 1915, was 26 per cent in the first year and 30 per cent in the second. The practical effects were for the LGOC to subsidise the railways, and for the management of all the Group railways to be integrated and consolidated.

Traffic grew throughout the war, for several reasons – members of the forces travelling across London, greater employment in London, and greater affluence, encouraging more leisure travel. Additionally, passengers preferred the Underground to the overcrowded and infrequent bus and tram services. The control of lifts from landings, instead of from each individual lift car, was first introduced at Piccadilly Circus on 8th January 1914, spreading to other stations, saving staff and giving a more regular service.

The Bakerloo extension from Paddington to Watford was completed during the war, but drew heavily on the Piccadilly Line's pool of spare rolling stock, to the extent of 67 cars by the end of 1919.

Trains became grossly overcrowded, even though all available rolling stock was pressed into service. From 1918 Government fuel restrictions required reduced evening services, reduced station lighting, earlier evening closure of some stations and some Sunday closures (including Down Street and York Road).

The Aldwych branch had started on its long downhill path soon after opening. A late night theatre express from Strand to Finsbury Park was withdrawn by the end of 1908. From that year the off-peak service was confined to the eastern platform at Holborn, but continued to Aldwych via the western tunnel south of the Holborn crossover. From 1912 the single peak train followed the same route as the off-peak. From 12th January 1918 the operation became 'one train on line' without signalling for the shuttle service. Strand was renamed Aldwych from 9th May 1915, and the line lost its Sunday service after 8th April 1917.

London experienced aerial bombardment (from Zeppelins and aeroplanes) from 31st May 1915 and during the periods of heavy bombardment people flocked to the tube stations for shelter. Air raids ceased on 19th May 1918.

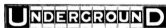
In 1919, London's passenger transport was in turmoil. A short-lived boom caused local transport to be overloaded, even more than in the war years. Rolling stock, tracks and roads suffered from lack of maintenance, and public sympathy had been forfeited by an Underground strike from 3rd to 9th February, and a general fare increase from 6th April. As a palliative, the LGOC introduced 180 lorry buses and some 'B'-type buses returned by the War Department, mostly painted khaki and labelled 'Traffic Emergency Bus'.

Public discontent caused London MPs to form a committee to consider London's transport. In May 1919 they heard evidence from Frank Pick of the reasons for service deficiencies and the causes of increased traffic and higher fares. On 29th May a Select Committee on Transport (Metropolitan Area) was appointed, under the chairmanship of W. Kennedy Jones, MP for Hornsey. The Committee heard evidence from the transport operators, including Frank Pick, but its main recommendation, for a Greater London Traffic Authority, was not acted on.

In October 1919 Pick published a report on possible road transport and Underground improvements for the next twelve years, including a new cross-London line utilising the pair of disused London and South Western tracks between Hammersmith and Turnham Green. Several proposals were made to extend tubes over main lines, and also the recurring idea of projecting the Aldwych branch to Waterloo. Other reports of the same period recommended better co-ordination and planning of London's transport, but the Government was too busy to tackle this complex problem. The post-war boom soon collapsed, and in 1921 national unemployment reached nearly two million. The Government's response was a Trade Facilities Act, offering a Treasury guarantee of capital and interest on works to relieve unemployment.

An air-door fitted all-steel car built for the Piccadilly in 1921 by Cammell Laird. Hand operated sliding doors were provided for movements between cars, as visible in this view.
LT Museum

At the end of 1912, there had been a little-publicised experiment with a four-car train on the Piccadilly, whose gate-stock bodies were converted to have pneumatically-operated middle and end doors. By 1914 it had been converted to manual operation, but one motor car was further adapted to work singly on the Aldwych shuttle. The sliding middle and end doors were mounted outside the body, and were opened or closed by wires wound on to a capstan at the trailing end. Driving equipment was also added at this end, so that the car could be driven from either direction.

In July 1919 the Underground Group ordered 40 all-steel cars for the Piccadilly from Cammell Laird of Nottingham. Originally these were to have end platforms, hinged steel gates and swing side doors, but by September 1919 the specification had been changed to air-operated, remotely-controlled sliding doors, with two centre doors flanking a thick pillar, each giving a 2ft 9in opening, and two sliding end doors with a 2ft 0in opening. When open, the doors slid into pockets behind the seats. The car interiors were finished in spartan fashion, with the 44 all-longitudinal seats being covered in leatherette and lacking armrests. No straps were provided for the standing load, but there were horizontal grab rails above the fronts of the seats and vertical rails on the draught screens flanking the doorways and part way along the rows of seats (stretching from floor to ceiling). The driving ends of the control trailers had oval windows. The internal livery was brown below waist level, white above, and the exterior was Derby red all over. Two features which were discontinued soon after the first train entered service were black and yellow external flapper arms which projected at right angles when any door was open, and a sensitive door edge which reversed the movement of a closing door if it touched an obstruction (including a last-minute passenger). All cars measured 51ft 4ins over coupler faces. Lighting was by pairs of clear bulbs in white frosted shades, in twin fittings on the ceiling. The air doors allowed an immediate saving in staff. On a six-car train there were two guards and a driver – three staff compared with six on a six-car gate-stock train.

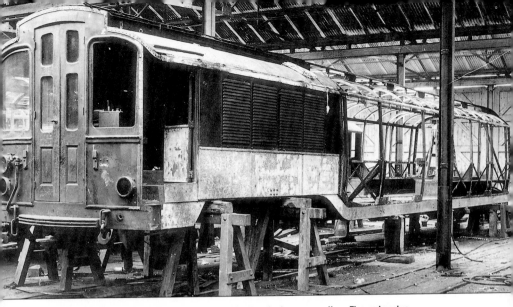

A French gate-stock car undergoing conversion to air-door operation. The extensive demolition of the passenger saloon demonstrates why it was not practical to convert the whole fleet to air doors.

Two French gate-stock motor cars were converted to air-door operation by Cammell Laird, and the first complete train entered service on 9th December 1921. The other 18 French motor cars were converted by the Gloucester Railway Carriage and Wagon Company. Conversion was slow, and the last air-doored train entered service on 20th December 1923. New trailer cars which arrived before converted motor cars were ready were stored in the disused eastern tunnel of the Aldwych branch.

In 1924 it was decided to modernise these cars with transverse seats, moquette upholstery and more attractive internal decoration, but after one car had been converted, the scheme was deferred until 1931. Meanwhile there was a need for new tube stock for the modernised City & South London Railway and the Hampstead line's extension to Edgware. Five rolling stock manufacturers were asked to build sample cars with two 4ft 6in aperture double air-operated doors per side, and 48 seats. The sample cars were formed into two trains and demonstrated on the Piccadilly from February 1923. They were used on the Hampstead line from August 1923. Soon afterwards the initial 191-car orders were placed for what later became a huge fleet of 'standard stock', numbering 1466 cars at its maximum.

With this ever-increasing Underground fleet, there was insufficient space at depots to undertake car overhauls, and the first section of a centralised overhaul works at Acton began work in December 1922. This had a direct rail connection to the District. The Piccadilly cars could reach the works via Hammersmith, the Central via Ealing Broadway, and the Bakerloo via Willesden Junction, Addison Road (Olympia) and Earl's Court. However, the Hampstead/CSLR complex was still isolated, and a new single-line tunnel was built at King's Cross, linking the northbound City line and the eastbound Piccadilly. This was completed on 27th March 1927, allowing cars from the Hampstead network to be moved to Acton via the Piccadilly Line, instead of being laboriously transferred by road vehicles.

A 1925 experiment in refurbishing a Cammell Laird interior to resemble a new standard-stock car as nearly as possible. The remaining cars were not converted until 1931.
LT Museum

The Piccadilly Line timetable required 27 trains for the peak service, and from December 1923 operated a mixture of original 1906 gate stock and ten Cammell Laird trains with sliding doors.

Railway rolling stock typically lasts for 40 years, and the gate stock was relatively young. In 1925 a Hampstead gate stock trailer was converted with revolving single doors at one end and sliding air-operated doors in the centre and at the other end. It ran on the Piccadilly for a short time before returning to the Hampstead. In 1927 one gate-stock car was sent to Birmingham and eight to Feltham for experimental conversion to air doors, but cutting the apertures for the door openings and door pockets in the steel body frames called for so much reinforcement to maintain structural strength that the conversion was not financially viable compared with the alternative of buying new stock. A decision to order Standard Stock as replacements was made later in 1927. At first these orders were placed in a piecemeal way, made more complicated by moving stock between lines and by the gradual change from a standard 6-car peak train formation to a standard 7-car. As the longer trains included a four-car set with a motor car at each end, only one control trailer was needed in each

A six-car train of Piccadilly Line standard stock with a motor car built by the Union Construction Company of Feltham in the lead. This view was taken at Lillie Bridge, which was the Piccadilly Line depot until 1932. LT Museum

train instead of two. Also, some trains were known as 'block trains' and were not shortened for off-peak service, so did not need control trailers.

In 1927 an order was placed with the Metropolitan Carriage, Wagon and Finance Co. for 136 cars for Piccadilly gate stock replacement, but some were later moved to the Hampstead line. There was a separate 1927 order for 20 motor cars from Feltham works to replace the French air-door motor cars in the Cammell Laird trains, and another order was placed with Feltham in 1929 to replace 53 cars of the 1927 batch which had been diverted to the Hampstead. In 1930 the Cammell Laird stock was thoroughly modernised and ran in this form on the Piccadilly between new standard stock motor cars before being transferred to the Bakerloo between January and October 1932. This transfer was balanced by trailers from the Bakerloo.

The first complete new trains of standard stock entered service on the Piccadilly in January 1929, and the transformation was so swift that the weekend of 6th/7th July 1929 marked the end of the 1906 gate stock on that line, apart from the Aldwych shuttle, where two double-ended French sliding-door motor cars took over from the Hungarian car in 1930.

In the early 1920s, fares tended to see-saw with the rise and fall of inflation. After the April 1919 rise mentioned above, there was another in September, and in 1920 powers were obtained to make the minimum fare 1½d instead of 1d. Longer-distance tube fares were reduced from January 1923; the 1d minimum on the tubes was reintroduced on 1st January 1925. From June 1923 a start was made in introducing Underground/bus and Underground/tram quarterly and monthly season tickets, and the destinations covered by such tickets were quickly augmented.

Dividends on Underground railway ordinary shares were still pathetically low, and prospects worsened with the advent of independent bus competition, from 5th August 1922. In 1925, Ashfield argued that no further tube extensions were possible, beyond those already in hand, without a Treasury guarantee and curtailment of bus competition.

In 1924 the London Traffic Act was passed. Its principal effects were to allow Government control of the volume of bus traffic along designated roads, and to establish a London and Home Counties Traffic Advisory Committee, with representatives from local authorities, police, government, labour and transport operators. In March 1925, the Minister of Transport asked the committee to examine the transport situation in three areas of London where there was great public dissatisfaction. The first review was of north and north-east London, where attention concentrated on Finsbury Park. Here there was heavy interchange between the two tubes (Great Northern & City and Piccadilly) and the bus and tram routes serving the areas further north.

Pressure to extend one of the tubes north of Finsbury Park had first arisen in 1919, and a petition containing 30,000 signatures had been delivered to the Ministry of Transport in June 1923. The organiser drew public attention to the 'veto' on tube extensions in the Great Northern's Act of 1902, and urged local MPs to vote against an LNER bill then going through the Commons. (At that time, the LNER had an annual General Purposes bill). By the following year the LNER had been compelled to agree to waive the veto or proceed with its own suburban electrification scheme; such a scheme was abandoned by November 1925.

The inquiry began in October 1925, and took evidence on the difficulty of finding space on a northbound bus or tram from Finsbury Park in the evening peak. It also heard from Frank Pick that the greatest weight of bus or tram traffic was via Harringay and Wood Green. The existing Piccadilly peak service of 24 six-car trains per hour had ample capacity. The inquiry concluded in the following month, and its March 1926 report recommended that the Piccadilly Line be extended to Manor House, with a special tube/tram/bus interchange, and that the LER be invited to explore a further extension to Wood Green or Southgate. The official LER response was that nothing could be done unless capital could be raised on reasonable terms, and bus competition curtailed. In practice, it quietly proceeded to survey an extension and to buy any suitable property which came on the market.

Away to the west, there were the almost-disused Southern Railway tracks between Studland Road Junction (just west of Hammersmith) and Turnham Green. The whole line between Richmond Junction (on the West London Line, about half a mile north of the present Kensington Olympia) and Richmond had been opened on 1st January 1869. Two extra tracks were opened between Studland Road and Turnham Green in 1911. The southern pair was used by the District and the northern by the London & South Western, but the LSWR abandoned the passenger service after 3rd June 1916. As mentioned above, Pick had plans in 1919 to use these abandoned tracks, and 1921 saw plans to incorporate them into a Central London extension to Richmond. However, in 1926, the 1913 proposal to extend the Piccadilly Line was revived, as the District was coming under pressure from the effects of housing development in Ealing, Hounslow and Harrow. A comprehensive agreement with the Southern Railway was made in 1926, for the Underground Group to use and staff the four tracks and stations between Studland Road and Turnham Green, and powers were also obtained to add two extra tracks to the District between Turnham Green and just beyond Acton Town. Again, a start of work had to wait until the financial problem had been solved.

In the centre of London, the westward shift of entertainment, office and shopping facilities had greatly increased the number of passengers using Piccadilly Circus station, but the existing surface ticket hall could not be extended as it was hemmed in by other buildings. If escalators could replace the lifts, they would provide greater capacity, allow a more even flow of passengers, and save staff. Therefore the bold step was taken to seek permission to excavate a large space under the Circus itself, and equip it with ticket offices, ticket machines, stairwell entrances from all the surrounding streets and escalators to the Bakerloo and Piccadilly Lines. The Eros statue was removed from the central road island, and an 18ft wide, 92ft deep working shaft was sunk, from which all the construction work was done. The roadway was supported by a network of steel girders, and service mains were diverted away from the ticket hall site. When the new station was officially opened on 10th December 1928, the opulence was breathtaking. Showcases, telephone booths and shops were framed in bronze, with a frieze and skirt in Travertine marble, and the lighting columns were finished in red scagliola. Five escalators led to an intermediate landing, whence three more served each line. The old station closed on 21st July 1929, and an arcade of shops was built on the site.

Formally opening the new Piccadilly Circus station on 10th December 1928, the Mayor of Westminster, Major Vivian B. Rogers, switches on an ornamental reading lamp and concurrently starts the escalators, assisted by Lord Ashfield on his right. LT Museum

Extensions at Both Ends

In 1929, with unemployment again increasing, the new Labour Government passed the Development (Loan Guarantees and Grants) Act in July. Unusually, it not only allowed the Treasury to guarantee the interest on capital raised for major works to relieve unemployment, but also to grant interest for up to 15 years, i.e., a direct subsidy. The Underground group submitted an application for assistance on 29th October. The proposed works comprised mainly Piccadilly Line improvements: a 7⅔ mile extension from Finsbury Park to Cockfosters via Wood Green, Arnos Grove and Southgate, a 4½ mile extension from Hammersmith to Northfields, parallel to the District, and reconstruction of many central and suburban stations.

Parliamentary powers had to be obtained for these works, and the London and North Eastern Railway was the most vocal opponent. The Underground Group contended that the LNER would not suffer, because the Cockfosters extension would be halfway between their lines, and the Underground served the West End while the LNER served the City. The North Eastern again offered a suburban electrification scheme, but did not attract much sympathy, as its public image was of slow and dirty steam trains, and the public pressure for a tube extension across Finsbury Park could not be ignored. The Underground obtained its Act on 4th June 1930, and construction could begin.

Left **The site of Arnos Grove station in October 1930. The Underground Group tried to keep the public happy by pretending to let them choose names, but it is doubtful whether public opinion had much real influence.**
LT Museum

Right **Joining the old running tunnel with the new, north of Finsbury Park, on 19th March 1931.**
LT Museum

The working site at Jolly Butcher's Hill, Wood Green. The tunnel segments are stacked on the left. This site was later occupied by a substation.
LT Museum

On the tube section from Finsbury Park to Tewkesbury Terrace, Bounds Green, this followed the normal sequence of serving notices on property owners, acquiring and demolishing property, sinking vertical shafts (at nine sites) and driving running tunnels by shields from the bottom of the shafts. Twenty-two shields were used, and the excavated soil was removed to the Lea Valley by a fleet of six-wheeled steam wagons with tipping gear. Some wagons brought back sand and gravel to make grout and concrete. Cast-iron segments were stored at Turnpike Lane and erected within the shields as tunnelling progressed. All tunnels had been driven by the end of 1931. On the open section, construction called for a 175ft girder bridge over the North Circular Road, a 95ft 6in road bridge outside the future Arnos Grove station, and a quarter-mile brick viaduct across Arnos Park. A half-mile tube tunnel section was built south of Southgate, and a further brick viaduct to the north. Stations and substations, signalboxes and Cockfosters depot followed quickly.

The first section, the 4.47 miles from Finsbury Park to Arnos Grove, opened on 19th September 1932, with intermediate stations at Manor House, Turnpike Lane, Wood Green and Bounds Green, all in tube. A total of 30,000 free return tickets to Piccadilly Circus were distributed to local residents. The 2.38 mile section from Arnos Grove to Oakwood (then Enfield West) via Southgate opened on 13th March 1933, and the final 0.81 mile to Cockfosters on 31st July 1933.

The practice of members of the Royal Family opening tube lines had fallen into disuse after 1900, but the Prince of Wales made a post-opening visit on 14th February 1933, travelling from Piccadilly Circus and inspecting Wood Green station and substation, as well as the Hyde Park Corner escalators on his return.

The cast-iron running tunnels were of the standard 11ft 8¼in diameter, widened to 12ft on curves of 1320ft radius or less. Bounds Green and Southgate station tunnels were of 21ft 2½in internal diameter, but at the other tube stations 23ft 2½in was adopted because of expected heavier traffic. All tube stations were 385ft long, and were equipped with anti-suicide pits between the rails. The station walls and circulating areas were faced with biscuit-coloured tiles, but tile friezes round advertisement panels and in passageways had a characteristic colour for each station – blue for Manor House, orange for Turnpike Lane and Southgate, green for Wood Green and red for Bounds Green.

Lighting was by incandescent bulbs in glass fittings, fixed to the undersides of the soffits where the ceiling joined the tunnel walls.

A Royal visit. Lord Ashfield explains a point to the Prince of Wales on a fact-finding visit to Wood Green and Hyde Park Corner on 14th February 1933. LT Museum

Bounds Green northbound platform just before opening, showing typical signs and posters. One may wonder whether the 'not stopping at' spaces on the train describer were ever used in practice. LT Museum

Arnos Grove platforms in pristine condition, March 1933. LT Museum

Above **The classic Arnos Grove ticket hall, photographed soon after opening.** LT Museum

Right **Poster issued for the opening of the extension between Arnos Grove and Oakwood on 13th March 1933.** LT Museum

The surface station buildings were in a style designed by the architect, Charles Holden, following a tour with Frank Pick to see new architecture in Northern Europe, made in summer 1930. The most prominent feature of each surface station was a tall ticket hall, with curtain walls of red-brown bricks and steel-framed cathedral glass, capped by a wide concrete frieze and an overhanging concrete cornice. Holden's office had so much work that some stations were designed by other architects, to Holden's general style. Arnos Grove, with its drum-shaped ticket hall, has often been cited as the perfect Holden design, but Bounds Green (octagonal) and Turnpike Lane and Oakwood (rectangular) were of very similar style. Southgate was circular, but lower, and Wood Green, in a row of shops, had a single curved frontage. Manor House ticket hall was subsurface, linked to ground level by stairways, including two from special tramway islands east of the road intersection. Turnpike Lane also had two tramway islands with stairways, connected to the subsurface ticket hall by subways. Cockfosters was low-lying and unimpressive at street level, but the three-road train shed was noteworthy, with reinforced concrete piers and ribs supporting a central clerestory. The surface buildings were to have been incorporated into a much larger development, but this was never built. Arnos Grove was a three-road station with reversing facilities and sidings, and Wood Green had a 465ft tunnel siding north of the platforms, where a train could be reversed from eastbound to westbound.

Wood Green and Manor House each had three escalators, of the 'MH' type, and Bounds Green two. Turnpike Lane had three of the slower 'M' type, and Southgate two. Stations with two escalators had a fixed staircase between.

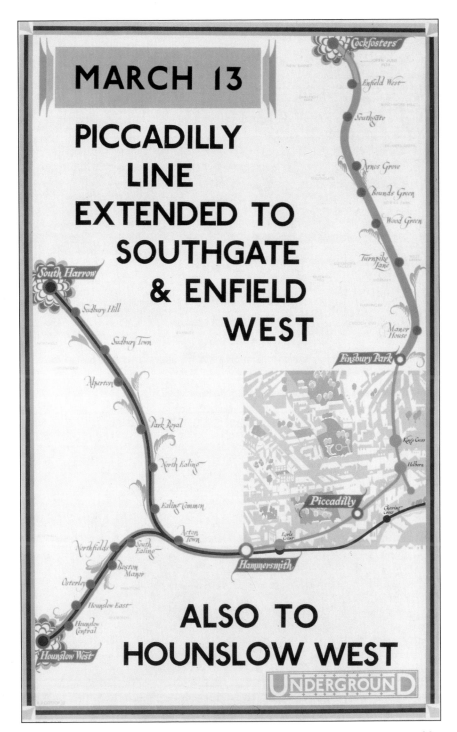

The north side of Southgate station in February 1934. The ungainly 'NS' type buses strike a jarring note. LT Museum

The southern ends of the isolated Southgate tunnels. LT Museum

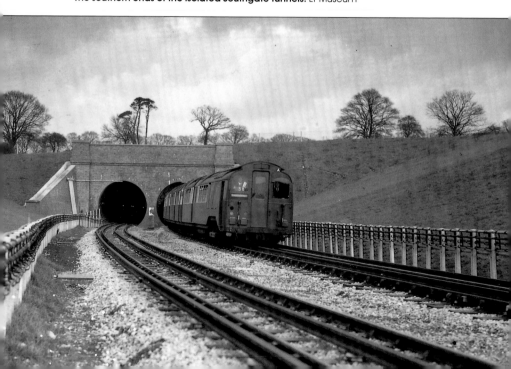

Turnpike Lane ticket office from Green Lanes. The stairs in the centre led to the sub-surface ticket hall. LT Museum

Cockfosters station. Train shed and ticket hall. Alan A. Jackson

At the western end of the line, the District was an old-established railway, having opened as far west as Hammersmith on 9th September 1874, and to Studland Road Junction (for a through service to Richmond via the London & South Western) on 1st June 1877. The section from Turnham Green to Ealing Broadway opened on 1st July 1879, and from Mill Hill Park (now Acton Town) to Hounslow Town on 1st May 1883, with Hounslow Barracks (now Hounslow West) being served from 21st July 1884.

Work was pressed ahead with equal energy to that expended on the northern extension, but in some respects was more complicated, as the District Railway service had to be maintained, and often rerouted on to new tracks. Proceeding west, the first major reconstruction was at Hammersmith, where a new railway underpass had to be excavated beneath Hammersmith Broadway, and a completely new station built with two island platforms, replacing the separate District and Piccadilly stations. Tracks had to be extensively rearranged between Barons Court and Hammersmith. Beyond the underpass, two new tracks climbed on either side of the disused viaduct that curved round to Shepherd's Bush, and linked on to the disused Southern Railway alignment at Studland Road Junction. Five arches of the curved section were demolished and replaced by a concrete bridge, allegedly at the insistence of the War Department. The disused platforms at Ravenscourt Park and Turnham Green were rehabilitated, but as Stamford Brook platform had hitherto served only the southern pair of tracks, a new platform had to be built on the north side to conform with the new pattern of District Line trains on the outer tracks and Piccadilly trains, running non-stop between Hammersmith and Acton Town, on the inner. Beyond Turnham Green, two extra tracks were accommodated by widening the embankment and building extra bridges over Acton Lane and Bollo Lane. Chiswick Park station had to be completely rebuilt, with platforms on the outer tracks. There were extensive track rearrangements west of Turnham Green.

Work on the new viaduct west of Hammersmith, June 1932. The two high-level tracks are part of the disused Southern Railway line towards Shepherds Bush. The tracks running down the slope will be, respectively, District, Piccadilly, Piccadilly, District. LT Museum

Standard tube stock at the rebuilt Hammersmith station, 1932.

The extra tracks through Chiswick Park have been completed, and a Piccadilly train is trying out the centre roads between the District Line tracks on 28th June 1932, in preparation for the South Harrow extension on 4th July. LT Museum

From Acton Town to Northfields room was found for four tracks by widening the existing shallow cutting. The brick overbridges were demolished and replaced by longer steel girder bridges. Beyond Northfields, the westbound through track burrowed beneath a depot access track, but from Boston Manor to Hounslow West there was little change to the track formation, nor from Ealing Common to Rayners Lane, except for a new fan of six sidings south of South Harrow. This section took over the pioneer electric line opened by the District from Hanger Lane Junction (north of Ealing Common) to Park Royal on 23rd June 1903, and to South Harrow on 28th June of that year. South Harrow to Uxbridge belonged to the Metropolitan Railway, and was completed on 4th July 1904. Rayners Lane to Uxbridge had a steam-hauled service from this date, but there was no regular service from South Harrow to Rayners Lane until 1st March 1910, when District trains started to provide an infrequent shuttle service to Uxbridge.

Tube type rolling stock took over some local District workings to Hounslow West and South Harrow from 8th February 1932, but the first through tube service from central London began on 4th July 1932, when Piccadilly trains were extended from Hammersmith to South Harrow. Sixty thousand free tickets were issued locally to

A view of Sudbury Town being built, with the main buildings on the eastbound platform.
LT Museum

advertise the extension. On the Hounslow branch, Piccadilly trains were extended to Northfields on 9th January 1933, and to Hounslow West on 13th March. The final part of the grand design for the Piccadilly fell into place on 23rd October 1933, when tube trains were extended from South Harrow to Uxbridge, making possible a 31¾ mile tube journey between Uxbridge and Cockfosters, taking one hour and 22 minutes.

The signalling on the original section of line was modernised, with track circuits converted from dc to ac, and additional signals installed. On the extensions, the standard Underground type was installed, with ac track circuits, colour lights, and the signal train-stops and points operated electro-pneumatically. Exceptionally, pneumatic semaphore signals were installed between Barons Court and just west of Chiswick Park to conform to the existing District arrangements. New signalboxes were provided at Cockfosters, Oakwood, Arnos Grove, Wood Green, Hammersmith, Acton Town and Northfields. In order to prevent a full-sized train attempting to enter the mouth of the tube tunnel at West Kensington, a gantry holding three mercury-filled 'U'-shaped glass tubes was built just west of Barons Court. A full-height train would break the tubes and set to danger the eastbound Piccadilly home signal at Barons Court.

Very large buildings were constructed for the substations, to the same general architectural style as the stations. The new mercury-vapour steel-tank rectifiers were an innovation of which little experience had been gained, as they were pioneered at Hendon Central in December 1930. There were new substations at Cockfosters, Southgate, Arnos Grove, Manor House, Chiswick Park, Northfields, North Ealing, Alperton and Sudbury Hill, with extra equipment in the existing substations at Acton Town and Ravenscourt Park.

Between Oakwood and Cockfosters, west of the running lines, a new car depot was built from steel stanchions and stock bricks, its exterior harmonising with the new stations. It had three eight-car tracks in the cleaning shed and nine in the maintenance shed. North of the depot were the stabling sidings for 250 cars. A similar depot was built west of Northfields, south of the running tracks, with a 19-track car shed and 19 open sidings. There was also a separate two-road lifting shop. Lillie Bridge depot was made over to the permanent way department.

Cockfosters depot from the south end, with the cleaning shed in the foreground and the through running tracks to Cockfosters on the extreme right. LT Museum

Many of the western suburban stations to be served by the Piccadilly were wholly or partly rebuilt. Hounslow West had new street-level buildings in Holden's Morden line style, with grey granite up to door height and Portland stone facings above. Vertical window panes were assembled into horizontal windows which allowed natural light to enter just below the ceiling of the heptagonal ticket hall. The new facilities opened on 5th July 1931.

The District station at Thornbury Road, named 'Osterley and Spring Grove' was replaced by a new Osterley station on the Great West Road in the new Holden style. There was a 70ft brick tower surmounted by a lighting column with individual lamps behind pressed-glass lenses. The ticket office and platforms were single-storey, with low clerestories. The new station opened on 25th March 1934, as did the rebuilt Boston Manor street-level buildings, which were generally similar. Here a brick lighting tower was capped by a smaller tower finished in biscuit-cream faience, and the lighting column gave the impression of one continuous light.

Northfields had to move to the eastern side of Northfield Avenue to make room for access to the new depot, and the four-track station, with two island platforms, was built in typical Holden brick box and concrete-lid style, with a deep forecourt and large ticket hall. A temporary ticket office south of the tracks was used from 19th May 1932, serving the new platforms, but was not required for railway purposes after the permanent ticket office opened on 18th December of the same year. An auxiliary ticket office was opened on the west side of Weymouth Avenue and reached from the east ends of the Northfields platforms by stairs, bridge and elevated walkway. This was part of the scheme to close or resite South Ealing station, but the scheme was withdrawn amidst local opposition, and the auxiliary ticket office closed permanently in 1942.

The widening from two tracks to four between Acton Town and Northfields entailed the replacement of the old overbridges by new bridges twice as long, and the consequent removal of South Ealing's buildings at street level. This photograph shows the 'temporary' ticket office about to take over from its predecessor. LT Museum

On the South Harrow branch, the stations between South Harrow and North Ealing were little more than corrugated-iron huts, and needed complete replacement. At Sudbury Hill the Holden design was adapted to an awkward site where the railway was in cutting, and was completed in 1932. Sudbury Town, built on an ample site in a commanding position at the end of an approach road, was the first full development of the Holden style. A large, tall rectangular ticket hall gave level passenger access from the forecourt, past the passimeter ticket office to the eastbound platform. A concrete footbridge connected to the westbound platform, which had its own exit and auxiliary ticket office. Unusual features included a refreshment room and barometer. Work began in December 1930, and the new station opened on 19th July 1931. At Alperton the railway was on embankment, and the rectangular ticket hall at its foot opened in 1932.

The existing 'Park Royal and Twyford Abbey' station was in an inaccessible side street, Twyford Abbey Road. On 6th July 1931 a new temporary station was opened on Western Avenue, named plain 'Park Royal', and the old station closed. Ealing Common was rebuilt in a similar style to Hounslow West, and was notable for a central triangular passimeter booth, including passenger-operated ticket machines, which could be serviced by the ticket clerks from inside the office. At platform level, passengers were protected from the elements by one of Holden's first clerestory platform roofs. The new facilities were opened on 1st March 1931. Acton Town was in the brick and steel-framed-window style, with a large rectangular ticket hall, and a long single-storey facade to a second entrance in Bollo Lane. There were five platforms, including a short one for the District's South Acton shuttle. North of the station the station tracks led to an impressive layout of flying and burrowing junctions, giving non-conflicting routes to and from Ealing Common and Northfields.

Charles Holden's masterpiece at Sudbury Town nearing completion. It opened on 19th July 1931. LT Museum

Hammersmith had complete new reinforced-concrete platforms, canopies and stairways, and a high-level covered way to the exit. The ticket hall was enlarged, but the 1906 facade to Broadway retained. An entrance from Queen Caroline Street, in Holden style, opened in 1934 after the main station reconstruction had been completed in 1932. For the Great Church Lane entrance, there were separate stairs, footbridge and ticket office.

Further east, the Earl's Court lifts were converted to fully automatic operation from 9th October 1932, but at Knightsbridge there was a bold and imaginative reconstruction, including a sub-surface ticket hall and two escalators at the Knightsbridge/Sloane Street junction, opened on 18th February 1934. A separate western entrance, with a ticket hall beneath Brompton Road and a shop-lined arcade from Hans Crescent, opened, with two escalators, on 30th July 1934. This allowed Brompton Road station to be closed permanently on the previous day.

The next station, Hyde Park Corner, had similar but less ambitious treatment, with a subsurface ticket hall at the eastern end of Knightsbridge, and two escalators flanking a fixed stairway. As at Knightsbridge, this enabled the existing lift-served buildings to be closed, together with an adjacent station. In this case Down Street was the victim, open for the last time on 21st May 1932, with the new Hyde Park Corner opening on 23rd May. A new 836ft tunnel siding, facing east, was built west of Down Street, and opened on 30th May 1933.

The Green Park station scheme also allowed the closure of another lift-served station in a side street, the 1906 Dover Street. The original Green Park platforms were served by two escalators and a fixed stairway from a ticket hall beneath Piccadilly, which had separate entrances from the north and south sides of that thoroughfare. The modernised station opened on 18th September 1933.

At Holborn there had been a long-standing problem of interchange with the Central London Railway, whose British Museum station was about 170 yards further west, without any subsurface connection. Plans had been drafted for an interchange subway as early as 1907, and parliamentary powers obtained in 1913 to move British Museum station to Kingsway. New powers were obtained in 1930, and the crux of the scheme was to construct new station tunnels around the existing Central London running tunnels. The project also included replacing the existing LER lifts with escalators, and enlarging the ticket hall at Kingsway/High Holborn. The complete scheme embraced four parallel escalators from street level to an intermediate landing (which had subway and staircase access to the Central London) and three more to an intermediate Piccadilly landing, as the platforms were on different levels. The Piccadilly part of the scheme was completed on 22nd May 1933, when '(Kingsway)' was added to the name, and the Central London on 25th September. By 1938 the volume of interchange traffic was ten times that of the former interchange at street level.

The little-used York Road station closed after traffic on 17th September 1932. Arsenal (Highbury Hill) was renamed from 'Gillespie Road' upon the suggestion of the team's general manager, Herbert Chapman, from 31st October 1932. Acquisition of the property next door enabled the ticket hall to be doubled in size and a wider subway to be built; these were finished by February 1934.

When the Cockfosters and Northfields/South Harrow extensions were approved, far more rolling stock was needed to cover the greater mileage. With the trend for greater distances between stations, there was a requirement for higher speed and better ventilation, whilst large door openings were needed to reduce station boarding and alighting times.

For a brief period in the 1930s, line identification was carried by standard stock. Photographed in December 1934, this is a trailer of 1931 stock. LT Museum

Following its earlier empirical approach, the Underground Group ordered another experimental train, of two motor cars and four trailers, the last tube stock to be built at Feltham. It was similar to the earlier standard stock, but the motor cars were 1ft longer (at 50ft 9½in over headstocks) and the trailers 2ft longer (at 51ft 9½in over headstocks). Two of the trailers had two double doors per side, but with the opening increased from 4ft 6in to 5ft 2in. The other two had additional 2ft 5in single doors at the car ends, but retained 4ft 6in doors in the centre. The number of seats fell from 48 to 40, but there were two tip-up-seats at each car end. At the trailing ends of the motor cars, the hinged doors of the earlier cars were replaced by air-operated sliding doors which could be used by passengers in the absence of the guard. The cars carried posters to stress that their construction was 'all-British'. As usual, they ran on the Piccadilly Line for a short time before being transferred to the Hampstead.

275 cars were ordered for the extensions, of similar design to the motor cars and four-door trailers of the experimental train, comprising 145 motor cars from Metropolitan-Cammell, 90 trailers from Birmingham Railway Carriage and Wagon, and 40 trailers from Gloucester. Finally, in what proved to be the very last order for standard stock, 26 motor cars were ordered from Metropolitan-Cammell in 1934, to serve the Uxbridge extension. Complete trains were built up by taking advantage of the surplus of trailers created by earlier policy changes.

The Piccadilly had achieved a quite complicated service pattern, and both staff and passengers had to keep alert. Non-stopping of intermediate stations was practised all day except in the early morning. One train would non-stop Gloucester Road, Hyde Park Corner, Covent Garden, York Road and Holloway Road; the next would non-stop Brompton Road, Down Street, Russell Square, Caledonian Road and Gillespie Road; the third train would repeat the stopping pattern of the first, and so on. This must have caused confusion to occasional passengers, but the management thought it worth while for the saving in time of about half a minute for each station missed, and for its effects in equalising train loadings. In 1930 four morning peak trains ran non-stop from Finsbury Park to King's Cross. Most trains were six cars long in the peaks, three in the off-peak and on Sundays, but by 1930 some 7-car peak trains had been introduced. Twenty-four trains per hour ran all day on weekdays until the end of the pm peak, increased to 40 at the height of the peaks.

London Transport Takes Over

For the first few years after 1933, the formation of the LPTB had little noticeable effect on the Piccadilly Line, which had been so thoroughly modernised under the previous regime that little remained to be done. Some station improvements which had been begun before 1933 but which were completed after the Board was formed will be described in this chapter.

As early as October 1933, there was a peak service at 1½-2 minute intervals between Hammersmith and Wood Green, 2-4 minutes to Arnos Grove, 3-6 minutes to Oakwood and 7-11 minutes to Cockfosters. At the western end, there was a 2-4 minute service to Acton Town, a 10-minute to Hounslow (where the District continued to run), a 5-minute to South Harrow and a 15-20 minute to Uxbridge (supplementing the Metropolitan service from Rayners Lane). These headways applied to both the Monday-Friday and Saturday peaks. As the outer-suburban traffic developed, a better service was provided on the extended sections, so that the peak rolling stock requirement rose from 57 trains in 1933 to 75 trains in July 1939. Another attraction of the Piccadilly Line was the high average speed. That of all Underground Group railways was 18 mph, but from Piccadilly Circus to Hounslow West or Rayners Lane was 23.7 mph, and to Cockfosters 22 mph. The drawing power of the tube was increased by the network of bus feeder services, easy road/rail interchange facilities at stations, through single- and season-tickets between tube and road services (more comprehensive on the northern extension than the western), and tapering fares, i.e. fares from the outer stations that were charged at less than the standard rate for the mileage involved. When these attractions were combined with modern stations with an easy transition from street to platform, the public found the tube irresistible, and the London and North Eastern's worst fears of traffic losses were realised.

The Piccadilly Line openings came just one year before the height of the boom in building new houses for owner-occupiers in the Greater London suburbs (72,756 new houses in the peak year of 1934), and there was the same predominant reason for both developments – national unemployment and depression. The stock market crashes and lower returns on government securities had caused investors to put their money into building societies, which were awash with money and eagerly seeking to earn interest by lending it to house purchasers. Building trade workers swarmed to London to seek work, and the pool of unemployed labourers enabled employers to keep wages down. The slump had caused a drop in the price of building materials, and farm or park land could be bought fairly cheaply. House prices were at their lowest-ever levels, with an average figure of about £500 and the lowest about £395.

There were many things to stimulate the rush to live in the suburbs – the desire to stop paying rent, and to move away from the congested areas, combined with the reduced size of families and the relative prosperity of London compared with the rest of the country. Private-enterprise housing in Greater London averaged roundly 25,000 new dwellings a year in the mid-1920s, rising to 42,000 in 1930.

At Arnos Grove, the Piccadilly Line reached undeveloped areas, and, after a slow

Rayners Lane in the 1920s. Soon after London Transport was set up the station and the area were to be transformed. H J P Rutherford

start, the builders were hard at work on landed estates and parkland, laying out roads and building houses on every acre of spare land north of Arnos Grove, around Southgate station, and east, south and west of Oakwood. However, as Trent Park remained inviolate, there was little development at Oakwood north of Bramley Road/Enfield Road, and Cockfosters had to rely on development west of Cockfosters Road.

A wide range of houses was available. At Southgate, the agent and developer Hugh Davies was advertising houses at £595, but John Laing and Sons built superior homes for £1,000 or more. Hilbery Chaplin advertised three-bedroom houses on Cat Hill for repayments 'from' 12s 5d weekly. In west London, some housing development had been stimulated by the District Line, but, as in north London, the Piccadilly Line was fortunate to be extended at the time of the great upsurge in building. The Wembley borough area saw its population increase from 18,239 in 1921 to 121,600 in 1939, although the Piccadilly served only its southern fringe. Rayners Lane had hundreds of new houses on both sides of the line, partly due to the Metropolitan Country Estates development named Harrow Garden Village. This was mainly built by E.S.Reid, who sold houses between £895 and £1,350 in 1932. Ruislip and Ruislip Manor stations were surrounded by new houses on all sides, and there were some quite large developments at Eastcote, Hillingdon and Ickenham. A great swathe of new houses stretched on each side of the Piccadilly Line from Rayners Lane to South Harrow, and for many miles to the west. Sudbury Hill, Sudbury Town, Alperton and Park Royal attracted their share of hinterland development.

The Hounslow branch served centres which were mainly built up, but there was much scope for building on unoccupied pockets of land, or in areas served by bus feeders, such as Cranford, Heston and Lampton.

New housing construction in Greater London continued at a slightly less hectic pace through the rest of the1930s, until the outbreak of war in 1939 brought a sudden halt.

Where the new housing areas encircled a station, the effect on station usage was startling. Rayners Lane passenger usage rose from 22,000 in 1930 to four million in 1937, and Ruislip Manor from 17,000 in 1931 to 1.3 million in 1937.

On the Rayners Lane branch, some station modernisations remained to be completed. At South Harrow, a new group of sidings south of the station was brought into use in 1932, occupying the site of the original 1903 shed for District trains. There were five sidings for trains to stable, and one for trains reversing there. In 1934 work began on a new South Harrow station, at Northolt Road/South Hill Avenue. A reinforced-concrete bridge (south of the Northolt Road bridge) was rolled into position on the night of 15th/16th September 1934, and formed the roof of a new ticket hall beneath the tracks. The hall extended on each side to single-storey entrances; two wide covered staircases led up to the new platforms. The wide reinforced-concrete canopies were supported by the rear walls and by concrete columns, and the long platforms continued in the open air to the original station building. The new station, designed by Charles Holden, opened on 5th July 1935. Two unusual features were the market which occupied eight arches of the viaduct north of Northolt Road, and, a short distance further north, a spur from the viaduct into the South Harrow gasworks. Steam locomotives brought trains of coal wagons into the gasworks from Harrow via Rayners Lane. These movements continued until the gasworks closed from 4th April 1954.

Park Royal had been served by a temporary station on Western Avenue from 6th July 1931, but an impressive permanent station opened on 1st March 1936, as part of a comprehensive development of flats, shops and an establishment trading as the Park Royal Hotel. There was a 67ft brick tower to draw attention to the station, adjoining a 40ft diameter circular ticket hall with a brick and glazed wall and concrete roof. Covered stairways led down to each platform, connected by a covered footbridge. The architect was Felix Lander. The permanent station was named 'Park Royal (Hanger Hill)' on opening, but the suffix was dropped in 1947.

Park Royal station, permanent buildings, opened on 1st March 1936. The coloured drawing is by the architect, F.J.Lander. The station is seen from the eastbound platform.

The London Passenger Transport Act of 1933 included a scheme to pool the net traffic receipts of London Transport and the suburban passenger services of the main line railways. This enabled railway facilities in the London Transport area to be planned comprehensively, and in June 1935 a programme of new works was announced, with Treasury guarantees of interest on loans. The 1935-40 programme included massive improvements and extensions to the Bakerloo, Central, Metropolitan and Northern Lines, and station improvements on other lines.

The Uxbridge branch had been overwhelmed by the housing developments of the early 1930s, and most of the old Metropolitan stations were in urgent need of improvement. The phenomenal increase in the use of Rayners Lane station had outstripped the capacity of the Metropolitan's timber booking hut and corrugated-iron shelters on wooden platforms. A larger, temporary wooden ticket hall was in service from 14th March 1935, and work began on a typical Holden-style brick and glass rectangular ticket hall, designed by R.H.Uren. The platforms, fences, light columns and stairways were reconstructed in reinforced concrete; on the eastbound platform there was a waiting room and a kiosk. The new station opened on 8th August 1938. A little earlier, a runaway ballast train had demolished the signalbox east of the station in the early morning of 22nd November 1934, and a new box at the Uxbridge end of the eastbound platform came into full use on 17th November 1935, with a new central reversing siding west of the station.

Further west, Eastcote station was rebuilt, and opened in May 1939 with a usual box-type ticket hall, resembling a smaller version of Northfields. At Ruislip Manor, the railway was on viaduct, and after a new 60ft girder bridge had been erected over Victoria Road in May 1936, a new station in the Holden style was opened on 26th June 1938, with a spacious ticket hall behind the bridge abutment.

Rayners Lane ticket hall, opened 8th August 1938 crosses the tracks where, a few years before, there had been just a small wooden hut. LT Museum

Uxbridge station, a three-road terminus, opened on 4th December 1938, replacing the inconveniently-sited station in Belmont Road. LT Museum

The Uxbridge terminus, opened by the Metropolitan in 1904, was hidden away in a back street, Belmont Road. It had but two passenger platforms, with principal station buildings on one platform only – the other platform had merely a small shelter. A bold scheme was clearly needed, and was achieved in co-operation with the local authority. A new 836-yard diversion line was built in a cutting with concrete retaining walls. It led into a new three-road terminus at street level, ending in a curved brick facade, behind a new semi-circular forecourt fronting on to the High Street, used as a bus layby. The three tracks, serving four platforms, were covered by an overall roof of glass and concrete, of similar design to the Cockfosters train shed. At the 'town' end of the ticket hall were three stained glass panels by Ervin Bossanyi, depicting the coats of arms of Uxbridge Urban District Council and the counties of Buckinghamshire and Middlesex. The new station opened on 4th December 1938. Design was by L.H.Bucknell in association with Holden. At that time, the Piccadilly Line peak hour service to Uxbridge was of 8 trains per hour, and in a full day there were 176 Piccadilly trains and 138 Metropolitan.

The largest and most intricate station improvement scheme carried over from the Underground company was the reconstruction of Leicester Square. The construction of a sub-surface ticket hall and the installation of three escalators for the Piccadilly and three for the Morden-Edgware were in some respects more complicated than the earlier Piccadilly Circus reconstruction, as the lifts penetrated the site of the new station. Charing Cross Road and Cranbourn Street were both narrow, and not more than half the carriageway could be taken out of use at once. Work had begun in October 1930, but much time had to be spent on initial steps, such as diverting service mains and underpinning the surface station building, the Crown Hotel and the London Hippodrome. The three Piccadilly escalators, of the MH type, had a vertical rise of 80ft 9ins, claimed at that time to be the longest in the world. One of these escalators was hurriedly brought into service for one day on 27th April 1935, for Cup Final traffic, and all six escalators and most of the ticket hall on 4th May, in time for the Silver Jubilee celebrations, which lasted until 11th May. The perimeter of the circular ticket hall included shops, stalls and telephone booths. There were two street stairwells on the west side of Charing Cross Road and one on the east side, south of Cranbourn Street. Closure of the lifts enabled the final part of the scheme to be completed, with stairwells from Charing Cross Road (east) and Cranbourn Street (north). These were brought into use on 8th June 1936.

At Earl's Court, the 1932 conversion to automatic lift operation was supplemented, from October 1934, by a public address system to warn passengers by loudspeaker that the gates were about to close. This was actuated by a beam of light, a moving film strip, a photo-electric cell and an amplifier and control relays. The original 1911 escalators between the District and Piccadilly were replaced by modern MA-type machines in 1936. In conjunction with the new Earl's Court exhibition hall and indoor stadium opened in 1937, and sited west of Warwick Road, a scheme was implemented to extend the Piccadilly subway underneath District platforms 1 & 2 to continue under Warwick Road to two new escalators, rising to a new ticket hall in the basement of the exhibition building. There was also a new subway to the westbound District platform and additional stairs direct from the eastbound. The new facilities fully opened on 14th October 1937.

At the time Brompton Road station closed in July 1934, an alternative station entrance for Knightsbridge opened opposite Harrod's, linked to the ticket hall by an arcade and escalators.
LT Museum

The Underground railway facilities at King's Cross bore eloquent testimony to the unplanned and unco-ordinated nature of the original railway proposals, with three sets of ticket offices and two sets of lifts. Reconstruction of King's Cross had featured in the plans for the 1930-32 new works, but was deferred because of the worsening financial situation, together with plans for an escalator station at Russell Square. With the advent of the 1935-40 New Works Programme, work started early in 1936. The principal feature of the tube part of the scheme was the excavation of a new circular ticket hall beneath the main line railway forecourt and approach road, to serve the Piccadilly and Northern lines. Three MH-type escalators descended 56ft 6in to Piccadilly platform level, where an extended circulating area had been excavated between the eastbound and westbound platforms. From the foot of the Piccadilly escalators a passage led to two MY-type escalators for the final descent of 18ft 6in to the Northern Line platforms. The tube part of the scheme opened on 18th June 1939. The Piccadilly Line station had 'for St Pancras' added in 1927, and became 'King's Cross St Pancras' in 1933. The Piccadilly surface buildings survived as shops and a staff canteen, but were demolished in 1963 for construction of the Victoria Line.

Control of train operation, and coping with emergency situations, are the main tasks of the line controllers, but over the years opinions have changed on whether it is better to have all the line controllers in the same building or at separate locations. In 1938 concentration was favoured, and a scheme was started to have all the controllers together in Cranbourn Chambers, above Leicester Square station. They had moved in by 1940, but the full scheme was not completed until 1948-9.

Another problem on which opinions changed over the years was that of noise absorption in the tubes. At first, attempts were made to retain the noise within the bogies. Shrouded bogies were tried, but found not practical, and instead body sides were lined with asbestos, the hazards of which were not fully appreciated. At the end of 1931 an asbestos mixture was sprayed on Piccadilly tunnel walls as an experiment, and in 1932 500ft of the eastbound tunnel between York Road and Caledonian Road was lined with 1½in asbestos mattresses, held on rods. Running rails welded into greater lengths also helped, and eventually a standardised continuous shelf at car floor level was evolved. Experiments were made with sealed windows and forced air ventilation on rolling stock but without success.

The performance of 'standard stock' had been enhanced in the early 1930s by introducing electro-pneumatic brakes and 'weak field' control for higher line speeds, but it retained the disadvantage of an equipment compartment on each motor car which occupied a car length of about 10ft not available for passengers. The floor of the equipment compartment was higher than that of the passenger saloons, in order to allow for the height of the traction motors, and the solution to the problem had to be pursued with two parallel developments – smaller traction motors which would fit under the passenger saloon floors, and redesigning and relocating the equipment such as control gear, resistances and compressors beneath the floors in the spaces not occupied by the bogies. By January 1935 such ideas had been developed sufficiently for preliminary designs to be drawn up, and for six cars to be ordered in June 1935. To assist with the motor clearance problem, the car floors were raised 4 inches above the motor bogies, and ramped down to the floors in the rest of the car.

Eventually 24 cars of what was subsequently known as '1935 stock' were ordered, with Metropolitan-Cammell supplying the bodies, underframes and bogies. Four different electrical manufacturers supplied their own designs of underfloor control gear. All cars were semi-permanently coupled in two-car units, sharing some auxiliary

1935 stock with streamlined front at Acton Town. The round fronts soon fell out of favour and the prototypes spent only a few years in service in this form. Capital Transport Collection

equipment. All cars were driving motor cars, with one motor per bogie, and 18 of the 24 had 'streamlined' or bull-nosed ends, with the driver occupying a special central armchair-type seat with 'joystick' controls. The odd six cars had flat ends, although the roof ends and body corners were neatly rounded.

The first of the 1935 stock trains entered service on the Piccadilly Line on 8th April 1937, and the last on 10th March 1938. Initially this stock worked as 4-car trains in the midday normal period, but six-car trains ran during the evening peak from 26th April 1937, with an extra two-car unit being coupled on at Northfields depot. The flat-fronted cars entered service on 24th January 1938, but were transferred to the Northern Line for gauging trials between March and July 1938. As there was such a large amount of experimental equipment in the 1935 stock, breakdowns were frequent, and a standard-stock train often had to be substituted. A six-car train of flat-ended 1935 stock had 252 seats (6 x 42), compared with 254 seats on a seven-car standard stock train made up with three trailer cars of the four-door type and one control trailer.

The PCM (pneumatic camshaft mechanism) control system supplied by BTH proved the most reliable, and was included in the specification of a new fleet of 1,121 cars, known as '1938 stock' including driving motor cars, non-driving motor cars (with motors but without cabs) and trailers. This stock had a similar external appearance to the flat-ended 1935 stock. The first orders were placed in March 1937, and the last in October 1938. From June 1938 the new trains entered service on the Northern Line, allowing some of the Northern's standard stock to be moved to the Piccadilly Line, where passenger traffic had increased by 60 per cent between 1934 and 1938, but the service had increased by only 24 per cent. The first benefits were seen in the Piccadilly winter timetable of 1938-9.

After the outbreak of war in September 1939, the Piccadilly Line traffic fell, and as the 1935 stock was still unreliable, all 24 cars were stored 'for the duration' from October 1940. The war had many other unwelcome effects on the line, as we shall see in the next chapter.

The Piccadilly Line in Wartime

The Committee of Imperial Defence had begun as early as 1924 to consider the role of Britain's railways during aerial bombardment. It was assumed that enough enemy bombers would be able to penetrate Britain's defences to destroy a large part of London. With the onset of dictatorship in Germany, air raid precautions were made more comprehensive and realistic. In 1937 the LPTB formed an ARP Committee and soon began taking practical steps to maintain its services under air attack. All staff were instructed in ARP, and many were formed into squads for rescue and demolition work, first aid and fire-fighting. Staff recruitment was planned to make up for staff enrolled in the forces, and all manner of special stores were bought, from the small tools for personal ARP work to the girders and heavy timbers needed to repair bomb-damaged tracks, tunnels, bridges and stations.

During the Munich crisis of late-September 1938, defences were hastily put on a war footing, and the respite until September 1939 allowed them to be strengthened and improved. On 1st September 1939 a blackout was imposed on civilian lighting, and the huge long-planned evacuation scheme for children and other vulnerable classes swung into action, taking four days to complete. Nearly 200,000 evacuees travelled from 72 Underground stations in the central area, to change at outer suburban stations to main line trains or LT buses to complete their journeys to reception areas. From 1st September 1939, all of London Transport's services, and those of the four main line railways and a few specified independent railways, came under government control, through the aegis of the Railway Executive Committee, which consisted of senior representatives of the five undertakings.

Another aspect of the emergency was the need to protect the Underground from flooding, principally from the River Thames, but also from broken water mains and sewers. As the Piccadilly Line did not cross the Thames, disruption was less severe than on the lines which ran in tunnels beneath it, where electrically-operated floodgates were installed to seal the under-water sections. However, some stations were closed from 1st September 1939 to instal watertight doors; King's Cross reopened on 17th November 1939, Arsenal, Green Park and Knightsbridge on 1st December, and Hyde Park Corner on 8th December. At some other stations, similar protection was installed without requiring closure.

The feared aerial bombardment of Greater London began at Croydon on 15th August 1940, but the major offensive began with the bombing of London's docks and much of the East End in daylight on 7th September, and during the following night. Then followed nightly raids on Greater London for 56 nights continuously. The single raid-free night of 3rd/4th November 1940 was followed by further heavy attacks on many nights until May 1941; from July, the Luftwaffe temporarily switched its onslaught to the Russian front.

Government policy on sheltering had been against providing deep-level shelters, fearing that people would enter such shelters and refuse to leave. The official line was that tube stations were not to be used for sheltering, but as soon as heavy raids began

Bounds Green surface station with its wartime accoutrements of blast wall and ducted air intake. LT Museum

Air raid protection at Knightsbridge station, built around the stairway on the north side of the road. LT Museum

the public flocked in, taking short-distance tickets and refusing to leave until the next morning. The maximum number of shelterers in tube stations was 177,500 on the night of 27th September 1940; in October 1940 the nightly average was 138,000. The authorities had to accept the situation, and stations were gradually made more habitable. Platform spaces were marked out and numbered, with admission tickets issued by London Transport in conjunction with the local authorities. Lines were painted on platforms to allow room for pasengers to alight from trains; three-tier bunks and sanitation facilities were installed, and special trains delivered light refreshments at lunchtime each day, to be warmed up and sold to shelterers in mid-evening or early morning. The numbers of shelterers varied with the intensity of bombing, and some stations were closed for sheltering during lulls in the air war. The last night of sheltering was 6th May 1945, and the equipment was removed as quickly as possible.

Most of the Piccadilly stations that had been closed in the early 1930s found wartime uses. Down Street was equipped for the Railway Executive Committee, but was sometimes taken over by the War Cabinet during the heaviest raids. At Green Park, the deep level passages of the old Dover Street station were fitted out for the London Transport chairman and principal officers, whilst Brompton Road was used as an anti-aircraft artillery command centre. Special suites of offices were also fitted in disused low-level tunnels at South Kensington, Knightsbridge, Hyde Park Corner and Holborn. The Aldwych branch closed after traffic on 21st September 1940, and had ample accommodation for sheltering and treasures from the British Museum, as well as offices and dormitories for LT staff.

The deep-level tubes were not entirely safe from aerial bombs and there were several instances where a bomb penetrated deep enough to damage the tunnels. The only recorded incident causing loss of life on the Piccadilly was at Bounds Green on 13th October 1940, when a bomb demolished two houses north of the station and brought down the roof of the north end of the westbound platform. Nineteen shelterers were killed and 52 injured. Normal services across Bounds Green were not resumed until 16th December 1940. On the night after the Bounds Green incident, the running tunnels at Holloway Road were severely damaged, and services between Wood Green and King's Cross were not resumed until 5th December. Incidents later in the war included bombing at Green Park on 11th January 1941, in which two LT staff were injured, incendiary bombs in the Gloucester Road lift shafts on 20th February 1944, damage to the viaduct near Ravenscourt Park in February and June 1944, and a bomb on the embankment near Alperton on 2nd March 1944, which caused services between Acton Town and South Harrow to be suspended until 7th March. For those who had to travel daily through nearly five years of aerial attack, the uncertainties of where the next blow would fall, and the delays and frustrations resulting from even minor incidents, probably had a more depressing long-term effect on morale than the individual major disasters.

The war caused some noticeable worsenings of travelling conditions. At first the blackout restrictions were very severe, and trains running on open sections were allowed only three small lamps in each car. However, after protests, special safety reading lamps were installed in December 1939 and January 1940. In 1942 lighting was reduced in trains and stations to save fuel, and the last nightly trains ran half an hour earlier. In the following year 24 stations had their down escalators stopped in off-peak hours and on Sundays. In order to reduce injuries from flying glass splinters, all passenger windows on cars were covered with a textile mesh held in place by a very strong varnish. Small diamond peep-holes were cut for passengers to see their stations.

Bomb damage at Bounds Green, westbound platform, when a bomb penetrated from the surface and killed 19 shelterers, also injuring 52, on 13th October 1940. LT Museum

After peace returned, the pattern of the mesh could be detected on windows for many years.

As in World War I, passenger traffic built up steadily during the war years, and there was acute congestion at interchange stations and those serving main line termini. Service frequencies were increased as far as resources allowed. As a rough indication of the volume of service, the July 1939 Piccadilly timetable had called for 75 trains on the 'main line'. This had dropped to 66 when through services were resumed after bomb damage, but had risen to 78 in October 1944.

Peace finally came to Europe on 6th May 1945, but London Transport had suffered some grievous blows, and restoring the well-planned, confident, tidy and reliable Underground environment of the Ashfield/Pick era was a task of awesome magnitude.

Mixed Fortunes

A symbolic return to normal living, and a step towards a brave post-war future, took place on the westbound Piccadilly Line platform at Piccadilly Circus on 2nd October 1945, when fluorescent lighting of the station tunnel replaced incandescent, giving three times the light. The conversion of the rest of the station soon followed, and, over the following decades, the whole Underground system changed to using more efficient light sources.

Politics and national austerity combined to dampen the prospects for any major Underground investment. The LPTB was swept into the nationalised transport system. From 1st January 1948 it became the London Transport Executive of the British Transport Commission, with all major decisions being taken at the higher level. In November 1947 Lord Ashfield left London Transport to serve on the BTC, but died one year later. One benefit of the merger was to transfer to London Transport the management and control of the erstwhile Southern Railway tracks and stations between Studland Road Junction (Hammersmith) and Turnham Green, with formal change of ownership following in 23rd January 1950. However, the broad effect was that London's needs were measured against those of the other national transport undertakings, particularly the run-down British Railways, and so rarely justified high priority. In a sense, London Transport was penalised for its high level of investment in pre-war days, and had to mark time until the other systems caught up.

There was a 1947 proposal for an additional interchange escalator and subways at Holborn, and a bold 1949 scheme for a 28-train depot at Ickenham, four-tracking between Acton Town and North Ealing, and a burrowing junction at Rayners Lane. All failed to obtain financial approval, as did a worthy 1965 scheme to extend the Aldwych branch to Waterloo. One minor scheme that was implemented was an extra low-level interchange subway at Leicester Square, opened on 5th July 1948.

Initially the volume of traffic on the Underground's main lines held up well, but some of the lightly-used sections came under scrutiny. The Aldwych branch was reopened on Mondays to Saturdays on 1st July 1946 (no Sunday trains had run after 8th April 1917). However, its service was reduced to peak hours only from 9th June 1958, and the Saturday service last ran on 16th June 1962. In summer 1958 an application was made to close the branch completely, but this was refused. In the far north-west suburbs, the Piccadilly began its long retreat from the Uxbridge branch, with the withdrawal of the Monday-Friday midday service from 2nd March 1959, followed by the Monday-Friday evening, and Sunday all-day service from October 1967. District trains were withdrawn from the Hounslow branch after 9th October 1964, and consequently Piccadilly trains ceased to be stabled at Ealing Common, and District at Northfields.

From the opening of the Piccadilly Line, two bare telephone wires had been installed through the running tunnels, enabling the driver to attach a handset to speak to the substation attendants to ask them to turn off the traction current. Later, this cut-off was achieved automatically by merely pinching the wires together or attaching the

The westbound Piccadilly Line platform at Piccadilly Circus just after being fitted with fluorescent lighting in October 1945. LT Museum

handset. Messages about emergencies had to be routed through the substation attendants. In 1946-7 a system was devised for a driver to speak directly to the controller by clipping independent connections to the tunnel wires, and using the train telephone microphone. Known as 'DRICO', this system was installed on all Underground lines by 1956.

The resignalling of the Uxbridge branch, completed in stages in October and December 1948, increased its capacity to 30 trains per hour. On the central section of the Piccadilly, a scheme to increase line capacity was introduced in 1949-50. Known as 'speed control signalling', this involved installing extra home signals before stations, with detection equipment preventing a signal from clearing unless the speed of an approaching train had been reduced to a predetermined level. The speed became progressively lower as the train neared the station ahead. This reduced the adverse effect on service regularity of an individual train having a lengthy station stop, as a second train could draw into a station as soon as the first had left. The new system was installed on the eastbound track between Green Park and King's Cross, and on the westbound between Finsbury Park and Piccadilly Circus.

The last semaphore signals on wholly-owned LT electric lines were replaced by colour-lights at the junction north of Ealing Common on 21st November 1953, when the South Harrow line signals were modernised.

A system which effectively signalled trains from the timetable, employing devices known as 'programme machines', was introduced on the Northern Line between 1958 and 1969, and on the western section of the Piccadilly Line, beginning in July 1965. This was completed on the central and western sections by October 1979. South Harrow was removed from control by Rayners Lane (introduced 1957) and placed under programme machine control in July 1978.

As mentioned earlier, all 24 cars of the 1935 stock were withdrawn in 1940 because of unreliability. A plan that was originally devised to augment the Bakerloo, Northern and Piccadilly lines was approved by the British Transport Commission in February 1948, but was modified several times when a Bakerloo extension to Camberwell at first seemed likely but very soon became unlikely. As finally approved, the plan involved converting the 18 streamlined cars of 1935 stock to trailers, and buying 70 new non-driving motor cars and 21 trailers. These were similar to the 1938 stock, but had some more modern technical features, including equipment to drive the motor cars for short distances from the vestibules, during the shunting operations needed to run shorter trains in the off-peak periods.

The net effect of these changes was to yield 15 trains of 1938 stock for the Piccadilly Line, releasing standard stock for the Central Line. The first 1938 train entered service on the Piccadilly on 12th November 1951 and the last on 15th November 1953. As a partial solution to the consequent problem of the 1938 stock being held up by the less powerful standard stock, the 1938 trains were timetabled to run in sequence in the direction of the heaviest peak flow, and the performance of the newer trains was at first downrated. The six non-streamlined cars of 1935 stock had their equipment modernised and were used on the Aldwych shuttle from 17th May 1954 until August 1957. Previously, the shuttle had been operated by a double-ended ex-gate stock motor car with externally hung sliding doors operated by capstan and wire. In 1930 this was replaced by a pair of French ex-gate stock motor cars with sliding doors, converted to double-ended configuration (i.e. driving equipment at each end). These cars were removed in 1940 when the line closed, and hauled the tube refreshment trains for a time. They reappeared at Aldwych on reopening in 1946, but were transferred to the service stock fleet in 1949 and replaced by a pair of standard stock motor cars. This stock provided the shuttle from 1949 to 1954 and again from 1957 to 1964.

The failure rates of Underground rolling stock, plotted graphically, follow what has been dubbed a 'bathtub' curve, with the failures of new stock falling rapidly as soon as the various initial problems are solved, then keeping at a low level until the stock nears the end of its working life, when failures rise again. By 1950 the oldest remaining standard stock was approaching the end of the curve, and plans were made for early replacement. These plans involved buying new trains similar to the 1938 stock, but had to be abandoned during the national economic crisis of 1952. However, stock replacement could not be deferred indefinitely, and in 1954 London Transport ordered one prototype seven-car train from each of three manufacturers. These trains, known as '1956 stock' began to enter service on the Piccadilly Line from 9th September 1957, the last on 14th April 1958. In general layout they were similar to the 1938 stock, but had unpainted aluminium bodies, rubber suspension, fluorescent lighting, roller destination blinds and door fault indicator lights. In conjunction with the Schoolboys Own Exhibition, London Transport demonstrated one of the new trains on seven non-stop round journeys between Acton Town and Hounslow West in the Monday-Friday midday periods between 1st and 10th January 1958. Souvenir tickets sold at the exhibition were priced at 1/- adult return, 6d child return (equivalent to 5p and 2½p).

Standard stock at South Harrow, where the original station building, taken out of use in 1935, remains intact half way along the eastbound platform. Alan A Jackson

A prototype 1956 stock alongside 1938 stock in Northfields depot.
Capital Transport Collection

Orders for a whole new fleet of cars for the Piccadilly soon followed, for 76 seven-car trains of '1959' stock. The first train entered passenger service on the Piccadilly Line on 14th December 1959, but after the nineteenth delivery on 24th June 1960, troubles on the Central Line prompted a decision to divert the flow of new cars to that line. A new order was placed for similar cars for the Central, known as '1962' stock. As these were delivered, the balance of fifty-seven 1959 stock trains was gradually moved from the Central to its intended home, and finally the last standard stock train was withdrawn from the Piccadilly in July 1964. A three-car train for the Aldwych branch had been added to the 1962 order. The 1959 stock was very similar to the 1956, but there were some detail differences. Subsequently the 1956 stock was modified to be operationally compatible with the 1959 and 1962 stocks.

Exterior and interior views of 1959 tube stock.
LT Museum

There had been proposals for a new tube line between Finsbury Park and Victoria as early as 1937. These ideas were refined and developed over the years, to appear as 'Route C' in the London Plan Working Party report of 29th October 1948. This would have run from Edmonton, Angel Road to East Croydon via Tottenham Hale, Finsbury Park, King's Cross, Oxford Circus, Victoria, Stockwell, Brixton and Streatham. The proposal was further modified and curtailed, and powers were obtained in 1955 and 1956 to build a new tube from Walthamstow to Victoria. However, what was now called the 'Victoria Line' had to wait for Government financial approval, which was not given until August 1962. As nearly every station gave interchange with other lines, and cross-platform interchange was provided wherever possible, construction was extremely complicated, and it took nearly seven years, until March 1969, for the whole line to be opened between Walthamstow and Victoria.

The Victoria Line affected the Piccadilly in two main ways, traffic and stations. As the Victoria Line provided a faster route between Finsbury Park and King's Cross, it attracted traffic and so helped to relieve the Piccadilly's most heavily loaded section, between Finsbury Park and Holborn. Heavy traffic diversion was recorded between Manor House and Green Park, but there were lesser diversions as far as South Kensington and Turnpike Lane. At stations, the effects of building the new line were more immediately apparent. At Finsbury Park, new running tunnels were built to divert the westbound Piccadilly Line through the former northbound Northern City platform, for same-level interchange with the southbound Victoria Line which was to use the southbound Northern City platform. In the northbound direction, the northbound Victoria Line would use the station tunnel vacated by the westbound Piccadilly, again giving same-level interchange, this time with the eastbound Piccadilly. The 3,150ft westbound Piccadilly diversion came into service on 3rd October 1965. At street level, the ticket offices were moved to new, temporary sites. At King's Cross and Green Park, the principal changes affecting the Piccadilly were the enlargement of the ticket halls and the construction of low-level interchange subways, including an extremely long subway at Green Park.

The construction of the Victoria Line tended to siphon off nearly all the funds available for Underground capital investment, so schemes on other lines were of minor degree. Hounslow East had a new waiting room and canopy on the eastbound platform in 1964, and Turnpike Lane bus station had an overall roof in 1967. Other changes were attributable to property developers and had little direct effect on operations. Covent Garden station was covered with three floors of offices in 1963-64, and spare land was developed at Cockfosters to provide two new office blocks in 1965, whilst land adjacent to the road access west of Northfields station was used to provide a four-storey office block in 1962-63.

The London Transport Executive of 1948 finally expired on the last day of 1962, to be replaced on 1st January 1963 by a new London Transport Board, reporting directly to the Minister of Transport. By the end of the 1960s, pressure had grown for London Transport to come under control of the Greater London Council, and this took effect from 1st January 1970, when a second London Transport Executive succeeded the Board.

A short piece of Piccadilly track at Turnham Green had been used by steam-hauled coal trains en route from Brent (Cricklewood) to goods yards at West Kensington and High Street, Kensington, but this ceased from 30th July 1965 when West Kensington yard closed. Freight services on the Uxbridge branch (calling at yards at Hillingdon, Ruislip, Eastcote and Rayners Lane), ceased from 10th August 1964.

New Trains and a New Market

In 1966 the British Airports Authority had direct talks with British Railways and London Transport about a rail link for Heathrow Airport, and in the following year a study group favoured a BR scheme for a north-facing spur from the Feltham-Staines line. London Transport used all possible arguments to persuade the decision-makers that a Piccadilly extension from Hounslow West was a better investment, and in May 1970 the matter was clinched when another study group favoured the LT scheme. Approval by the Greater London Council followed in July, and Government approval in November. At first the only external funding promised was 25 per cent of the capital cost by the GLC, but the Government finally agreed to provide another 25 per cent in 1972, leaving LT to find 50 per cent.

Map showing the alternatives proposed by London Transport and British Rail for links to Heathrow Airport. The BR scheme found favour initially but the Piccadilly Line extension eventually won the day.

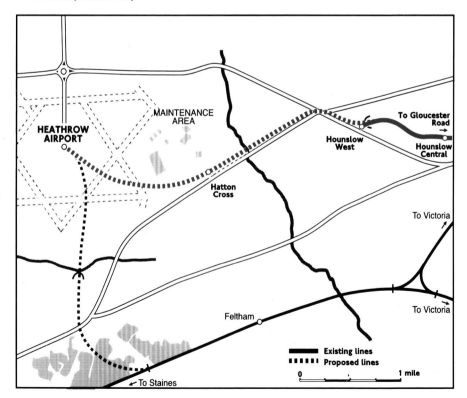

The official start of work was on 28th April 1971, but some work had begun a little earlier. The new line was to begin just before the existing Hounslow West station, to serve a new island platform just below ground level, connected to the 1931 ticket hall by stairs and a covered passage. From here to the first station, Hatton Cross (1.81 miles) the new line was made by cut-and-cover construction, beneath the verges of the Bath Road and the Great South West Road. On the last-mentioned section it climbed to surface level to cross the small River Crane by bridge, giving overseas visitors their first close glimpse of London outside the airport. Beyond the bridge, it descended on a 1 in 48 gradient to the subsurface Hatton Cross station, another example with an island layout, connected to the surface buildings by stairways. Shortly after Hatton Cross, the line plunged into twin 12ft 6in tubes lined with concrete segments which continued to just before the central area. Here was a 31ft 2in tunnel for the scissors crossover, and final short lengths of tube brought the trains into Heathrow Central station, 1.34 miles from Hatton Cross. The station was built in a giant concrete box, 400ft long, 80ft wide and 50-60ft deep, constructed in the open air and later covered over. The two tracks served each side of a wide island platform, connected to the ticket hall by four escalators. From the ticket hall, separate travolators in mainly horizontal subways took airline passengers directly to Terminals 1, 2 or 3, and two escalators and a fixed stairway led to a modest surface-level building adjoining the bus station.

Cut and cover construction on the Heathrow extension immediately west of Hounslow West, under the service road parallel to the Bath Road. Desmond Croome

A huge civil engineering operation over the weekend of 11th-13th July 1975 allowed the two Piccadilly tracks to be rerouted via the new Hounslow West station, which opened on 14th July. Trains continued empty to Hatton Cross to reverse, and this station opened on 19th July. The complex construction work at Heathrow Central took a further 2½ years, but the extension was finally opened by Her Majesty the Queen on 16th December 1977. With the help of plentiful – and ingenious – publicity, passenger traffic increased swiftly, and 25 million passengers used the extension from opening date until February 1981 (about 3¼ years). A passenger count of Heathrow Central users totalled 7.6m in the depressed year of 1981, short of the predicted figure of 11m, but traffic later built up steadily, with the Piccadilly retaining its 20 per cent share of air passengers arriving or departing from Heathrow. Trains ran every 4/5 minutes in the peaks, and never less frequently than 7½ minutes at other times. The average running time to Piccadilly Circus was 40 minutes. The extension became an essential part of the London Underground network, and one may wonder how London ever managed without it and why its construction was delayed so long.

By the beginning of the 1970s, the huge fleet of 1938 stock tube cars and compatible types was beginning to approach the end of its working life. Some mitigation was given by the delivery of 63 trains of new 1972 stock in 1972-74, but more cars were needed. With the Heathrow extension set to go ahead, it was highly desirable that Heathrow should be served by a fleet of new trains, for several reasons – to create the impression of a modern railway, to improve speeds and braking, to provide more space for passengers' luggage, and to provide for eventual one-person operation, which, until then, was confined to the Victoria Line. The new stock would allow the 1959 stock on the Piccadilly to move to the Northern Line to replace 1938 stock. Therefore a proposal was approved by the GLC in November 1971 to buy 87 6-car trains and one 3-car of what was later known as '1973 stock'. The one-person operation requirement determined that the overall train length should be reduced, to allow greater leeway to bring trains to a halt in the tunnel stations. Therefore the design embraced six-car trains of cars which were individually about 6ft longer than the 1959 stock, making an overall train length of about 350ft, or 17ft shorter than a seven-car train of the older stock. Each 6-car train comprised two 3-car units of motor-trailer-motor. Twenty-one units had driving cabs at both ends, the others at one end only. Internally, there were cross seats in eight pairs between the double doors, but the other seats were longitudinal. The screens by the double doors were set back to allow space for passengers' luggage, and, at the car ends, the vestibules by the single doors were made larger for the same reason. A complete train provided 264 seats, compared with 288 on seven cars of 1959 stock. Perhaps the most important technical innovation was the 'Westcode' braking system, which applied the brakes by compressed air but controlled them by electric circuits.

Upper right **Hounslow West station being resited underground, with the original ticket hall visible in the background. 12th July 1975.** Desmond Croome

Right **The giant 'box' for Heathrow Central station, under construction in 1976.** Desmond Croome

Technical problems delayed the trains' entry into public service, but one train was ready for the official Hatton Cross opening in July 1975, to be returned to the depot for a further month afterwards. Apart from trains retained for crew training and for experiments, all the 1973 stock was in service by 18th October 1979, allowing the 1959/62 stock on the Piccadilly to be released for other lines. At an earlier stage, the last 1938 stock on the Piccadilly ran on 2nd December 1975, and it was thus able to visit Hatton Cross for a few months.

Above
Hatton Cross station nears completion in its month of opening, July 1975.
Capital Transport

Left
1973 tube stock at Southgate.
Capital Transport

Above
With Her Majesty the Queen in the cab alongside J Graeme Bruce, a train of 1973 stock formally opens the Heathrow extension, 16th December 1977.
LT Museum

Left
Her Majesty being shown the operation of the push-button journey planner at Heathrow.
LT Museum

In 1974 the GLC approved a 10-year programme to replace all the remaining Edwardian lifts and all pre-1940 escalators by modern equipment. Installing new lifts was normally accompanied by retiling work at the upper and lower landings. Piccadilly lift stations to benefit from this programme comprised Holloway Road (2 new lifts completed in March 1984), Caledonian Road (2 in July 1985), Russell Square (3 by 1985), Covent Garden (2 in 1987 and 2 in 1989), Gloucester Road (2 in 1989), and Earl's Court (2 in 1982). The South Kensington lifts were replaced by a completely new installation of three escalators in a lower flight (September 1973), and two in an upper flight (January 1974). An improved ticket hall served the Circle, District and Piccadilly Lines from October 1973.

On the Uxbridge branch, Ickenham station was graced with a new small brick ticket hall, opened in September 1971, and resting on a concrete slab built over the tracks.

Following a successful experiment at Holborn from December 1962, closed-circuit television on platforms was installed throughout the Victoria Line (1968-1971) as original equipment, and in 1972 its installation was authorised for platforms of the other lines at Victoria Line interchange stations, i.e. King's Cross and Green Park on the Piccadilly Line. Public address systems were often installed at the same stations as the CCTV, and both systems were available on the Heathrow extension, followed by a 1978-80 group which included Piccadilly Circus. Public address was gradually extended to most stations on the network, with CCTV at heavily-used stations or those with serious crime problems.

Signalling and point operation for the terminal at Heathrow Central had been controlled by local computer from opening in 1977. The signalling on the central and western sections of the line was transferred to control by programme machines, monitored from Earl's Court control room, between 1965 and 1979. In 1982 computer-controlled signalling took over between Cockfosters and west of Wood Green, but initial problems experienced with this have still not been totally eliminated.

Radio communication between train drivers and the line controllers had long been available on most overseas Metro systems. London experiments began in 1972, with tall radio masts for open-air tracks and radio cables in tunnels. The Bakerloo Line was fully operational in 1977, and others followed, including the Piccadilly by mid-1985. Further devices designed to allow one-person operation comprised an automatic warning in the cab if the deadman's handle was released for more than a minute, and an automatic warning to the line controller if the handle was not then re-set. There was also provision for the line controller to speak directly to the train passengers in such circumstances.

The less onerous problem of introducing one-person operation on the sub-surface lines was overcome between 1984 and 1986, and the devices mentioned above allowed the regulating authorities to be convinced of the system's safety for the tubes. After effecting some rolling stock modifications, and with TV monitors or mirrors installed on platforms, one-person operation was introduced on the Piccadilly on 31st August 1987.

When the tubes first opened, each line had its own maintenance depot, where all maintenance was performed, ranging from daily cleaning and safety checks to long-term general overhaul. Between 1919 and 1920, 312 cars were added to the Underground fleet. With further large fleet increases planned for extensions and improvements, substantial extra space was needed. In December 1920 a decision was made to build Acton Works, west of the District and Piccadilly Lines between Chiswick Park and Acton Town, on market garden land. The first stage was built in 1921/22, and

1959 stock at South Harrow, with sidings on the left. John Laker

the first cars were overhauled in 1922. The works were progressively expanded to overhaul stock on all lines. They continued to overhaul all LT railway rolling stock until the end of the 1970s, but with modern stock designed to need overhauling at very long intervals, they had less work to do. It was found more economical to revert to the pre-1922 system of overhauls in depots. A new workshop was built at Acton to overhaul individual items of equipment, opened in September 1989, and an Engineering Support Unit Workshop at Ealing Common followed in 1990 for heavy repairs and major modifications.

Back on the operating railway, there had been some worrying events on the eastern end of the line. On 6th February 1976, the theft and earthing of a neutral lighting cable at Finsbury Park caused arcing in an escalator feeder cable. Five Piccadilly trains were halted, some amongst dense smoke. Twenty-five people were taken to hospital but none detained. On 16th March 1976, a faultily-timed terrorist bomb wrecked part of an empty train at Wood Green, which was due to pick up Arsenal football supporters a few minutes later. On 11th August 1982, a mishap at Cockfosters depot caused the positive conductor rail to be earthed, and the negative rail to carry 600 Volts. On a 1973 stock train just south of Bounds Green an arc developed between the negative rail and a loose bolt under the car, which was severely damaged resulting in 15 people being taken to hospital suffering from the smoke and fumes. The incident helped to speed up the installation of driver/controller train radio.

For many years, severe winter weather had disrupted Underground services, and many different methods were tried to overcome the principal problem – the formation of ice on the conductor rails, preventing the flow of current. By the early 1960s the standard methods were to have small baths of de-icing fluid in gaps in the conductor rail, to be spread by the trains' collector shoes, and also to use electric sleet locomotives (each formed of parts of two Central London 1903 motor cars) to break and remove the ice. In 1963 the practice of short-circuiting the negative and positive conductor rails was extended to the uphill side of the Piccadilly Line between Arnos Grove and Cockfosters. This raised the conductor rail temperatures enough to melt any snow or ice. Point heaters were also installed extensively to prevent blockage by snow. By the end of the 1960s the de-icing baths and sleet locomotives were being phased out in favour of fitting a proportion of the normal passenger trains with steel brushes and sprays for de-icing fluid, and this practice has continued on new stock. The latest standard for point heaters was to have electrically-heated pads between the chairs and sleepers.

The first few years of GLC control of London Transport were reasonably happy and unexciting, but in later years County Hall increasingly attempted to impose policies which might have been desirable in theory but whose long-term effects had not been thoroughly worked out. Relations between London Transport and the Conservatives gave rise to some bizarre and farcical happenings, but Götterdämmerung came with the arrival of a radical Labour administration at County Hall in May 1981, and the introduction of an overall reduction of 32 per cent in London bus and tube fares from October 1981, with some flat fare zones in central and inner-suburban London. As most of the GLC's income came from a precept on the London Boroughs, the borough ratepayers were unhappy at the extra burden. A legal challenge by the Borough of Bromley was followed through the successive appeal stages until, in December 1981, the Law Lords ruled the new fares illegal, resulting in a 96 per cent fare increase in March 1982. After the legal ruling had been considered in greater detail, it was found that some reductions were permissible. A fare revision involving an overall reduction of 25 per cent was introduced in May 1983, further extending the zonal principle. By now, the Conservative Government's patience was exhausted, and it wrenched control of London Transport from the GLC in June 1984, soon to be followed by the abolition of the GLC itself.

The higher rate of pay for drivers on the Victoria Line caused a mass movement of drivers from other lines, leading to a staff shortage which lasted until the middle of 1974. Matters worsened with a strike at Acton Works from October to December 1969, which interrupted the vital flow of overhauled rotary air compressors for 1938 stock. Some 7-car trains were temporarily reduced to 6 cars, and the Piccadilly had to return to the Bakerloo and Northern Lines 10 of its fleet of fifteen 1938 stock trains.

With these problems, coupled with two fare increases in 1975, and the increase in private motoring, overall Underground traffic declined from 3.32m passenger miles in 1972 to 2.275m in 1982. However, GLC policy was to keep the scheduled train mileage broadly unchanged, although staff and rolling stock shortages often combined to cause the actual service to fall well below the scheduled level. The Piccadilly Saturday service to Uxbridge was withdrawn from midday after 28th November 1970, and completely after 28th September 1974, leaving the bare minimum of a Monday-Friday peak hour service. Piccadilly trains began to call at Turnham Green on Sundays from June 1963, and late at night from October 1964. Over the years, Saturday services on all lines were gradually reduced, and Christmas Day services entirely withdrawn after 1979.

1973 stock train ascending the ramp just west of Hammersmith. The remains of the arches for the one-time Southern Railway line to Shepherd's Bush are on the left. *John Laker*

The severe fare increases of March 1982 were accompanied by proposals for heavy economies, including the closure of the Aldwych branch. Reduced peak hour services were planned for introduction on 22nd March 1982, but were delayed by strikes. A programme of reductions was then agreed with the trade unions, and the Piccadilly Line had a reduced service from 27th September 1982, losing 13 trains from the timetable. On 6th December five peak hour trains were restored.

From 29th June 1984 the administration of London Transport moved to a new body, London Regional Transport, appointed directly by the Secretary of State for Transport. In some respects this was the low point in London Underground's fortunes, but many of the benefits enjoyed in the early days of LRT control sprang from the development of policies initiated by the GLC.

Preparing For a New Era

The new, more business-orientated, London Regional Transport took over from the London Transport Executive on 29th June 1984, and three subsidiary companies were established. These included London Underground Limited, which began trading on 1st April 1985. A feature of the Act establishing LRT was the obligation to seek tenders from external companies for all work done in-house which could reasonably be made over to an external company or organisation. As the internal departments could submit competitive tenders, they were obliged to improve their efficiency. This process later developed into schemes known as 'Make or Buy', and the Government-inspired Private Finance Initiative which tended to be used for the larger projects.

Serving the ever-growing Heathrow Airport traffic kept London Underground's planners fully engaged. With the introduction of larger aircraft, the pressing need was for extra terminal buildings. After a 1978 public inquiry, the Government approved the building of Terminal 4, in the south-eastern sector of the airport, in December 1979. A working party considered every possible form of public transport to the new terminal. The scheme that would attract the largest proportion of air passengers to public transport was a single-tunnel Piccadilly loop, diverging from the present line at Hatton Cross, serving a new single-platform station at Terminal 4, and then swinging round in a large loop, eventually to split into two tunnels and make end-on junctions with the over-run tunnels at the then Heathrow Central station. The scheme was estimated to cost £27 million, with the Government funding about half, and the GLC and British Airports Authority one quarter each. As soon as the finance was settled, London Transport pressed for the loop to be completed at the greatest possible speed, and a formal start of work was made on 9th February 1983. Tunnelling was mainly in London clay, with conventional shields, but the lining was of precast concrete segments, each ring being forced together by hydraulic rams until there was room to insert two wedge-shaped keys. The main working site was at Wessex Road, near the Perry Oaks sewage farm. At Hatton Cross the new line diverged into a new shallow-level section, formed by building new retaining walls and demolishing a section of the existing wall. It continued for 230 metres in a cast-iron tube built in an open trench, where it linked with the concrete tunnel for the remaining 1,350 metres to the Terminal 4 station. The remaining tunnel drives were of 2,900 metres to the working site, and of 1,150 metres to the step-plate junction where the tunnel split into two. By 3rd November 1985 the new loop was equipped and signalled, and it was formally opened by the Prince and Princess of Wales on 1st April 1986, with the public opening following on 12th April. Heathrow Central station was renamed Heathrow Central Terminals 1 2 3 from 3rd September 1983, and the 'Central' was deleted from 12th April 1986.

A fifth terminal was proposed before the fourth opened, and there was a planning inquiry in 1984. In March 1986, consultants were commissioned to make a 'Heathrow Surface Access Study', and their 1987 report included numerous permutations of extensions to LT or British Rail lines. London Transport submitted a Piccadilly Express scheme, with a new tunnel from west of Hatton Cross to east of Osterley, two extra

The attractive platform at Heathrow Terminal 4 station. Only one platform is needed here as the extension was built on a loop. Capital Transport

tracks thence to Northfields, and a tunnel by-passing Acton Town. From the end of this tunnel the existing tracks would be used, to a new terminus at King's Cross. However, a separate Heathrow Express scheme, with overhead electrification of the exisiting BR main line from Paddington to a point west of Hayes, and a new tunnel to Terminals 1,2,3, and Terminal 4, found more favour. Work started in January 1992 and was completed in 1998. Terminal 5 would be served by both London Underground and Heathrow Express.

Nineteen years after opening, the ticket hall at Heathrow 1,2,3 was beginning to have a weary image. Some tidying up has been done, with more ticket machines, customer service staff, and better signs and sightlines. Ticket-issuing machines of improved design have been installed in the baggage reclaim hall of Terminal 1. Work was due to begin in 1998 on rearranging and improving the whole of the ticket-issuing facilities at this station and to be well under way in 1999.

At South Ealing a completely new ticket hall was built on the north side of the tracks, on the site occupied by the original station buildings until the 'temporary' ticket office of 1931 opened on the south side. The modern ticket office came into use on 3rd May 1988, concurrently with a new covered footbridge to all platforms.
Capital Transport

London Underground had for many years sought a system which automatically would check tickets on entry to the network and check or collect them on departure, and in 1982 the prototypes of what came to be known as the 'Underground Ticketing System' were installed at Vauxhall station on the Victoria Line. The system had three main elements: (a) complete reconstruction of ticket offices to give far greater security to the ticket clerks and to incorporate many long-needed improvements in accounting and accountability practices; (b) new self-service ticket-issuing machines for passengers, which could be restocked from inside the ticket office and (c) entry/exit gates at stations, initially installed at central area (Zone 1) stations only, but later extended to some other stations where traffic was heavy.

Reconstruction of ticket offices was a huge and intricate task, involving 247 stations in all. It lasted from 1986 to 1989, when Covent Garden had the final UTS ticket office on 1st July. The main programme of gate installation, at 64 stations in Travelcard zone 1, took from 1987 to 1990, and initially encountered some public opposition. One result of ticket office reconstruction was the disappearance of the 'Passimeter' or island-type ticket office, used extensively in the new or reconstructed stations of the 1920s and 1930s, but now deemed too cramped and insecure.

The 'listing' procedure for buildings of architectural merit (under which special permission is needed to make alterations) was first applied to Underground stations on 19th February 1971, when Arnos Grove, Oakwood, Southgate and Sudbury Town were so honoured. The process has been continued so that by 1994 fifty-seven Underground stations had been listed nationally or locally, of which 25 (or 44 per cent) were served by the Piccadilly Line, which expanded during Charles Holden's most creative period.

In 1981 the Greater London Council found an opportune seven-year gap in London Transport's planned expenditure on new rolling stock, and planned to fill the gap with a 10-year rolling programme of station modernisation. A total of 140 stations were included but two-thirds of the expenditure was allocated to 16 major schemes at heavily-used stations. At tube level, the station walls were retiled or fitted with vitreous-enamelled decorative sheets. Some stations were merely cleaned, repaired and repainted (as at Covent Garden, Gloucester Road (tube level), Knightsbridge and Russell Square) and Earl's Court was retiled in a neat, plain scheme of white and green. Gloucester Road had a new glass-roofed District and Piccadilly ticket hall from 14th January 1990, in conjunction with adjacent shopping and residential developments above the District tracks. Restoration of Barons Court to its 1916 condition was recognised by an Ian Allan National Railway Heritage Award on 5th March 1998.

Piccadilly Line stations with bolder changes of appearance included Finsbury Park (mosaic murals of hot air balloons – 1985); King's Cross (new black, white, red, green and blue tiles, forming the letters 'K' and 'X' – 1987); Holborn (enamelled panels representing exhibits in the nearby British Museum, and floors retiled in black and white squares – 1988); Leicester Square (blue tiles with white 'sprocket holes' for the local film offices and cinemas, and enamel plates with pictures of neon tubes – 1985); Piccadilly Circus (completely retiled in biscuit, green, red and blue, fitted with brass handrails – 1986; ticket hall renovated and some subways altered – 1989); Green Park (new tiling on the platform walls, in an irregular design of blue, pink and green – 1985), and subsequent works put in hand to cater for the extra traffic from the Jubilee Line Stratford extension, including a new station information room and a direct subway between the Jubilee and Piccadilly Lines; and South Kensington (new tiles with representations of extinct animals (westbound platform) or living (eastbound) – 1989).

Restoration of the heritage – Rayners Lane, dating from 1938 and recently refurbished, and the Yerkes style building at Gloucester Road restored to its original 1906 glory in 1998.
Capital Transport

The Hammersmith island site was the subject of a lengthy legal tussle between the developers and the local authority, but after this was settled, construction proceeded rapidly, and a long shopping arcade at ground level gave access to two separate ticket offices. There were escalators to a high-level bus station. Commercial offices ringed the site perimeter, and the District/Piccadilly platforms had completely new roofs and platform furniture, with one Bennie hydraulic lift (for the mobility-impaired) from each island platform to the west overbridge. The new main ticket office (north-west end) opened on 5th July 1993, the south-eastern ticket office on 12th September 1993 (both connecting directly with the shopping arcade), and the lifts on 5th July 1994. On the outer suburban sections of the Piccadilly, the stations from Turnpike Lane northwards were cleaned, repaired and repainted from 1985, with Southgate in particular having many of its original features sensitively restored. Station information rooms have been installed between Turnpike Lane and Caledonian Road, inclusive. Better interchange facilities with buses are being introduced at Wood Green under a 3-year programme.

The old Metropolitan Hillingdon station stood in the path of a planned diversion of the A40 London-Oxford trunk road, and a completely new station was built slightly nearer Uxbridge. The Cassidy Taggart partnership won a London Underground architectural competition, and the light and airy design included glass block walls in the ticket hall and two overlapping 'V'-shaped glass roofs covering the ticket hall and part of the platforms. There was a hydraulic Easton Elevator lift on each platform to convey the mobility-impaired to ticket office level. The new platforms were available from 29th June 1992 and the new ticket office from 6th December. The lifts were in service from 14th November 1994.

Turning to the train service, the Piccadilly had a spectacular 13 per cent increase in train mileage on 29th September 1996, when a daily off-peak service of 24 trains per hour was introduced for the trunk section, with Piccadilly trains running to Uxbridge daily. Station staff were given special training in despatching trains promptly. A further increase to 28 trains per hour in the peaks was planned for the completion of the 1973 stock refurbishment programme.

The new station at Hammersmith, completed in 1994. Capital Transport

The end of the Aldwych branch. The final departure on 30th September 1994. John Laker

Over the years, the question of closing the Aldwych branch had been raised on several occasions, but it lingered on until the need to replace the lifts could no longer be postponed. On 4th January 1993 London Underground announced that it was about to give formal notice of its intention to close the station. The closure proposal quoted a cost of £3 million to renew the lifts for an average of 900 passengers on each of the Monday-Friday days it was open. The economic case for closure was overwhelming, although the twin tunnels might have earned their keep if the line had been extended from Aldwych to Waterloo, for which parliamentary powers had been obtained in 1965.

The Secretary of State for Transport gave permission for closure on 1st September 1994, and the last train ran on 30th September. For many years the eastern platform tunnel at Aldwych had been used to display mock-ups of new ideas for station decor. The branch had also been used extensively whenever a tube train was needed in a new film, television drama or advertisement.

Several London area railway schemes may bring extra traffic to the Piccadilly, although their precise effects will not be known until they open. Completion of the high-speed Channel Tunnel rail link will certainly bring extra traffic into King's Cross/St Pancras, both from the Continent and from commuter country in Kent. The Piccadilly and Victoria Lines are likely to come under further strain if most of the new passengers wish to continue to central London and the West End. Thameslink 2000, with improved services on the Farringdon-Blackfriars section and a running connection with the Great Northern lines, may bring some extra traffic to Finsbury Park and King's Cross; the Jubilee extension to Stratford may bring some extra interchange traffic at Green Park. Heathrow Express, between Heathrow Terminals 1,2,3 & 4 and Paddington may initially divert some traffic away from the Piccadilly, but the airport traffic is constantly growing, and if Terminal 5 is approved, this source of traffic will doubtless make up for that lost to the new line.

Extensive plans are being made to handle the extra traffic, although, as is always the case, their realisation depends on sufficient inflow of investment capital.

Track quality and infrastructure have suffered from years of underinvestment, but a start was made with track renewal at Acton Town and embankment stabilisation on the Rayners Lane branch. At stations generally, the installation of more station information rooms will give station staff immediate notification of any developments, and so enable them to help passengers more quickly.

Taking some particular stations where new works would improve their ability to handle extra traffic, an extra platform at Cockfosters and another at Oakwood would help to handle a more intensive service. Finsbury Park has television monitoring/recording and a new control room, but long-term plans include a new ticket hall at intermediate level and new escalators or stairways. King's Cross ticket office would be enlarged as part of the works for Thameslink 2000 and the Channel Tunnel rail link. At Russell Square a larger ticket hall has been investigated, and long-term plans exist to rebuild Covent Garden with a new ticket hall to supplement the existing one. The traffic at Knightsbridge (west end) justifies a new ticket hall, although this may depend on external funding. At Hounslow East, plans have been prepared for a new ticket hall south of the tracks, with direct access to each platform. At Park Royal, interchange facilities to the Central Line have been examined, possibly including an extra Central Line station at Park Royal and moving the Piccadilly Line platforms north of Western Avenue.

Turning finally to rolling stock, the 1973 stock has to perform the treble functions of conveying Heathrow passengers and their luggage, carrying commuters between the suburbs and central London, and acting as an in-town distributor for passengers from King's Cross/St Pancras and from intersecting Underground lines. The line is heavily used by tourists between King's Cross and Earl's Court on every day of the week. As mentioned earlier, the 1973 stock was designed with large stand-back spaces by the double doors and extra-large end vestibules. By 1990 this stock was beginning to look shabby compared with refurbished stock on other lines, and it was time to have a further look at the provision of luggage space. A three-car unit was refurbished by Metro-Cammell by October 1990, with special luggage racks between the double doors, smaller cross seats, and various configurations of stand back areas, grab poles and rails. The three-car unit was coupled to a standard unit for passenger service, and began to carry fare-paying passengers from 20th January 1991. Extensive market research was carried out. At three locations passengers were asked to complete

Left **Interior of unmodernised 1973 stock, showing the inadequate provision for airline passengers' luggage.** Capital Transport

Right **One of the prototype revised layouts in the refurbished three-car unit which entered service in January 1991, showing a perch seat convertible to luggage space.**

questionnaires on the relative merits of the three experimental cars. Additionally, advertisement cards asked passengers to send in their views, and interior video filming gave useful information on passenger movement within the redesigned car.

A working group of engineers and users' representatives met to devise a list of desired features. Warwick Design were chosen to translate the ideas into an interior design and produce a full-size half-car interior mock-up, embracing 37 London Underground engineering standards. When the specification was agreed, the usual tendering procedure followed, and the contract was awarded to RFS Engineering of Doncaster on 5th May 1993. This company went into administrative receivership on 15th December of the same year, but was sold to Bombardier Prorail in April 1994, to which company LUL transferred the contract. When the programme at Horbury (near Wakefield) was in full swing, a train would pass through the works in six weeks, and there would always be four trains being modernised at once. The first refurbished train was 'launched' by the Minister for Transport in London on 17th June 1996, and the original refurbished unit was withdrawn for a new-style refurbishment in August 1996. The design was chronologically after that for the new Jubilee Line stock but before the new stock for the Northern Line. There were some similiarities between all three stocks. As happened with other renovated stock, the rehabilitation has been so thorough that passengers may believe they are travelling in new trains.

All cross seats have been replaced by longitudinal, reducing overall seating by 6 per car, but increasing standing capacity by 20 per car. There are large standbacks by double doorways, for luggage or extra standing capacity, with perch seats in these areas and at car ends. Interior dot-matrix passenger information (destination etc) displays are fitted and there is improved passenger audio information.

As smart and sleek as a new train – a refurbished unit of 1973 stock seen at Sudbury Hill.
Capital Transport

New interior panels of powder-coated aluminium or painted phenolic are mainly ivory above waist level, dark grey below. Vertical and horizontal grab rails are in 'Piccadilly Line' blue. New moquette-covered seats on phenolic pans can be raised *en bloc* and held up by gas-struts to allow access to equipment. Heating is by electric radiant panels at floor level. Floors are covered in wear-resistant rubber matting. Two new windows are fitted in each car end not occupied by a cab.

Below the floor there are new arc barriers to reduce the risk of fires caused by short circuits, made from resin-bonded reinforced woven glass. Aircraft-style honeycomb aluminium frames support the floor. Above the ceiling fully forced-air saloon ventilation is fitted, with seven fans per car extracting air from the saloon. Fresh air enters by units above the seats. Other rolling stock developments have included an overall exterior repaint in two-tone blue of one six-car train of 1973 stock for United Airlines, launched on 19th June 1995; the first such exterior advert on the Underground. Following trials on the Piccadilly Line, a programme of fitting inter-car barriers to prevent passengers falling between cars at stations began in 1998.

Soon after, design work was started to enable 15 trains of 1983 mark II stock, displaced by new Jubilee Line trains, to be refurbished to the same standard as the 1973 stock (including enlargement of the mid-car doorways), to run on the Piccadilly Line to augment the existing fleet of 87 six-car trains. With layout and signalling improvements, this will enable peak services on the trunk section to be increased to 30 trains per hour.

The Piccadilly Line has developed far beyond what can have been in the mind of David Lloyd George when he drove the first train from Hammersmith on 15th December 1906, and faces an exciting future.

Inside the modernised 1973 stock. Additional luggage space is provided alongside the double doors, with a fixed perch seat available when the luggage space is not needed. In the colour scheme, extensive use is made of Piccadilly Line blue. Capital Transport